WHAT GOD HAS SAID
—ABOUT

LENN ZELLER

*A Bible study for personal reflection
or small group discussion.*

What God Has Said—About Jesus
A BIBLE STUDY FOR PERSONAL REFLECTION
OR SMALL GROUP DISCUSSION
by Lenn Zeller

Copyright © 2021

All rights reserved. No part of this book may be used or reproduced by any means, graphic, electronic, or mechanical, including photocopying, recording, taping or by any information storage retrieval system without the written permission of the author except in the case of brief quotations embodied in critical articles and reviews.

This book is a work of non-fiction. Unless otherwise noted, the author and the publisher make no explicit guarantees as to the accuracy of the information contained in this book and in some cases, names of people and places have been altered to protect their privacy.

Because of the dynamic nature of the Internet, any web addresses or links contained in this book may have changed since publication and may no longer be valid. The views expressed in this work are solely those of the author and do not necessarily reflect the views of the publisher, and the publisher hereby disclaims any responsibility for them.

Scripture quotations taken from The Holy Bible, New International Version® NIV® Copyright © 1973 1978 1984 2011 by Biblica, Inc. TM. Used by permission. All rights reserved worldwide.

Library of Congress Number: 2021941880
International Standard Book Number: 978-60126-745-0

Masthof Press
219 Mill Road | Morgantown, PA 19543-9516
www.Masthof.com

DEDICATION

Sola Deo Gloria—*to God alone be the glory.*

Table of Contents

INTRODUCTION | vii

CHAPTER 1	*The Offspring of the Woman*	1
CHAPTER 2	*The Ruler of the Tribe of Judah*	11
CHAPTER 3	*The Spirit of the L*ORD *Will Rest on Him*	21
CHAPTER 4	*The Precious Cornerstone*	31
CHAPTER 5	*My Servant, My Chosen One*	38
CHAPTER 6	*Called and Kept*	47
CHAPTER 7	*The L*ORD *Our Righteousness*	56
CHAPTER 8	*The Sovereign Son of Man*	64
CHAPTER 9	*The Source of Our Peace*	73
CHAPTER 10	*The Beloved Son of God*	83
CHAPTER 11	*The Beloved Son of God—2*	92
CHAPTER 12	*Superior to All Others*	102
CONCLUSION	*The Testimony of the Father*	110

ENDNOTES | 115

ABOUT THE AUTHOR | 123

Introduction

My previous book was titled *What God Has Said—About God*, and it focused on Scriptural passages, all in the Old Testament, in which God made some kind of direct, self-revelatory statement about His own character and person. The premise was that if we want to have a true understanding and perception of who God is, and we certainly should (rather than the imaginations of our own hearts), there is no better place to turn than to God's own words about Himself.

A natural follow-up to that discussion would be a similar study of what God has said *about Jesus*, and that is the gist of this volume. Here we will again look at passages in the Bible where God has plainly said something about His Son, Jesus Christ. This time we will include verses from both the Old and the New Testaments, as there are statements from God about Jesus in both major sections of the Bible.

Perhaps a word about the Triune God would be in order here at the outset. It's true that Jesus is God, and God is Jesus; and the Holy Spirit is God and God is the Holy Spirit. The God of orthodox Christianity is a holy Trinity. The term "Trinity" is not itself found in the Bible, but there are three clear Biblical affirmations that have led to the historic doctrine of the Trinity: 1. There is but *one* God; 2. The Father, the Son and the Spirit is each fully and eternally God; 3. The Father, the Son, and the Spirit is each a distinct Person.[1]

How all three statements can be true at the same time, I cannot fully explain. A woman once left a church I pastored and went to join a false religion that told her God is one, not three. She had always struggled to comprehend the Trinity, and they played into her confusion to pull her into their cult. Alas, I was not able to explain the doctrine in a way that convinced her of its truth! But I firmly believe it because the Bible says it is so. Just another example to show that God is beyond human comprehension!

So to consider what God the Father has said about Jesus is essentially the same as to contemplate what God has said about Himself. And yet, there are three distinct Persons in the Trinity who relate to one another in some way as unique Beings. I would suggest therefore that it would be worth our time to look at some of the things that God the Father has said about Jesus the Son if we want to have a clear and true understanding of who Jesus is.

People have arrived at all kinds of different conclusions about who they think Jesus is: wise teacher, good man, spiritual guru, moral example, prophet, faith healer. Others, less charitable, have seen Him as a charlatan, liar, misguided fool, even mad. What matters is who Jesus is in truth. It is true that we are all entitled to our own opinion. But it is also true that our opinions can be wrong, and many are. What is the *truth* about Jesus? Who is He in actuality?

In this volume we will ask those kinds of questions of God Himself, turning to His eternal, infallible, universal Word of Truth for the answers. Some of the revelatory statements we will study are straightforward words directly from God. Others will be given through prophets speaking on behalf of God. But the Scriptures we will consider are ones in which God has spoken about His beloved Son.

I was involved in a conversation recently that turned to politics—gasp! It became quickly apparent that those involved stood at opposite ends of the political spectrum. What also became rather obvious was that a lot depended upon to whom you turned for your information. If you tend to listen to mainstream media opinions that are almost entirely to the left of the political divide and you consider them to be faithful and true to the facts, then your beliefs invariably fall in line with what that particular "news" outlet feeds to you. If you listen to and believe voices on the other end of that continuum, then your views again follow in that divergent direction.

The same is true theologically for your views about God—and about Jesus. They tend very much to be influenced by the sources you read, listen to and believe. Other religions and cults speak of Jesus, but their beliefs are radically different from Biblical orthodoxy. Even some who claim the name

"Christian" espouse views of Christ that are definitively awry and against the clear, historic teachings of the faith.

So to know for certain who Jesus really is we will turn to the one and only infallible source of information—God and His Holy Word. What kinds of things did *God* say about His Son? How did He affirm and encourage Jesus Christ? That's what we want to look at in this volume. Scripture gives us some great examples. In all such cases we will be contemplating reliable, consistent and trustworthy expressions of the person and character of Jesus Christ.

Please note that this small volume is not meant to be an extensive, systematic description of the Christ—His incarnation and humanity, His deity, His atoning sacrifice and resurrection. That is a much larger discussion that others have discoursed much better than I ever could. For a fuller description of the doctrine of Christ, a good place to start would be Dr. Wayne Grudem's *Systematic Theology: An Introduction to Biblical Doctrine* (Zondervan Publishing House, Grand Rapids, MI, 1994). There are many other similar works that define an orthodox doctrine of the Christ.

But it is imperative that we make every effort to have an accurate understanding of Jesus, the most compelling, preeminent and significant person to ever walk this earth. When United States astronauts first walked on the moon, the President at the time said, "The greatest event in human history was when man set foot on the moon." Not true! The greatest event in human history was when *God* set foot on earth, in the form of His only Son, Jesus. Let's look at some of the things God Himself told us about His Son.

CHAPTER 1

The Offspring of the Woman

"And I will put enmity between you and the woman, and between your offspring and hers; He will crush your head, and you will strike His heel." (Genesis 3:15)

Adam and Eve, the first humans, were in the Garden of Eden. They enjoyed a life of perfect harmony with creation, each other and most of all God. The Garden was free of weeds, predators and natural disasters.[2] They lived together in wonderful unity and closeness. On top of that, Adam and Eve daily walked in personal, intimate union and communication with God. It was an existence that we cannot even fully imagine. How that would not have been enough for them I have never understood. But they allowed Satan to convince them to seek more and they went after it. God had told them they were free to eat the fruit of any of the trees of the Garden except for one—the tree that was in the middle of the Garden—the tree of good and evil. But following the serpent's cunning and treacherous deception, they did just that.

Immediately discord entered their relationship with each other. When confronted by God, Adam quickly turned on Eve, justifying his disobedience by blaming her. "It was Eve's fault," he said. "She gave me the fruit and I ate it;" implying that she had somehow fooled him. She hadn't. He was right there with her the whole time and was a willing participant in her disobedience. The perfect union they had once enjoyed was gone!

Anyone who has been married for any length of time can relate. Yes, thankfully, there are times when the intimacy and oneness are glorious and the marriage relationship is everything we had ever hoped it would be. But there are other times when it just isn't working, when the discord is real and sometimes painful. And not only in marriage is this true. In all other human relationships there will be at least times of misunderstanding, disunity, and subtle and even open conflict. For many relationships that seems to be the rule rather than the exception. We still suffer the effects of the fall in our human relationships.

There was also a painful separation from God. Whereas they had once walked with Him in perfect oneness, they now hid from God among the trees in the Garden. They were afraid of Him, ashamed of their own behavior and fearful of His response. The perfect communion they had once enjoyed with God was also gone!

There, too, we all still deal with the aftershocks of Adam and Eve's sin. Paul talked in 1 Corinthians about how we now see *"but a poor reflection as in a mirror; then we shall see face to face."* (1 Corinthians 13:12) As fallen human beings our relationship with God is always, at least to a degree, clouded, distorted and unclear. We long for the day when that will finally be healed and we will be able to see Him face to face, relating to Him openly, without the cloud of our fallen sinfulness to get in the way.

God's judgment was swift and just. The serpent was cursed above all the livestock and animals (Genesis 3:14). It was condemned to a lowly life of slithering in the dust of the earth. There has been some debate about whether this was a literal serpent or some other type of creature that *became* a crawling snake as a result of God's wrath. The term used here—"serpent"—is *nachash* in the Hebrew. It has several possible meanings: "to hiss," "to whisper" (as in sorcery or divination), and even "to shine."[3] This has led some to believe that this was originally a beautiful creature of some sort that was punished by God in making it a thing to be detested and feared. At least, someone near and dear to me detests and fears them; which is an unfortunate circumstance as we now live in a place that is teeming with them!

Others point to the Arabic root of the word—"to creep"—to argue that it was indeed a serpent from the start. In either case, God's punishment was immediate and severe. Adam and Eve did not escape unscathed either.

To the woman He said:

"I will greatly increase your pains in childbearing;
with pain you will give birth to children.
Your desire will be for your husband,
and he will rule over you." (Genesis 3:16)

To Adam He said:

"Because you listened to your wife and ate from the tree about which I commanded you, 'You must not eat of it,' cursed is the ground because of you; through painful toil you will eat of it all the days of your life. It will produce thorns and thistles for you and you will eat the plants of the field. By the sweat of your brow you will eat your food until you return to the ground, since from it you were taken; for dust you are and to dust you will return." (Genesis 3:17-19)

In addition to that, Adam and Eve were banished from the Garden and cherubim with flashing swords were stationed to guard the entrance and keep the humans away from the tree of life (Genesis 3:24-25).

The effects and implications of these judgments were massive, however we will not take the time to discuss them in full detail. That would be a worthy study in itself. Suffice it to say—the disobedience of Adam and Eve had serious and far-reaching consequences not only for them but for all humanity to follow (and for all of creation itself). We live with those consequences to this day, on a daily basis. Life is hard. It's not at all what we were created for or long for deep in our hearts. We all know that something is wrong, that something is amiss, even if we can't express it or define it.

However, in the midst of these painful—but just—penalties, God also spoke a word of grace and hope. It was, in fact, His first spoken word about His Son Jesus, the Messiah, to come. In His judgment against the serpent, God had said:

"And I will put enmity between you and the woman,
and between your offspring and hers;
He will crush your head,
and you will strike His heel." (Genesis 3:15)

The reference there, most scholars seem to agree, was to the coming Savior, Jesus Christ. He was the offspring of the woman mentioned in that passage; the woman's seed, as other translations say it. Granted, it would be many centuries before that divine descendant would arrive, but the promise was already made in response to Adam and Eve's dreadful rebellion. Theologian R. C. Sproul used the term *"cosmic treason,"* and said that "the slightest sin is an act of defiance against cosmic authority. It is a revolutionary act, a rebellious act where we are setting ourselves in opposition to the One to Whom we owe everything."[4]

If ever there was a sin worthy of the term "cosmic treason" this was it. In fact there is an old legend which says that when Adam took the first bite of the "forbidden fruit" and tried to swallow, it stuck in his throat because he felt so guilty. Ever since, the slight projection at the front of the throat formed by the largest cartilage of the larynx, which is usually more prominent in men than in women, has been called the "Adam's apple."[5]

God responded with justified and righteous punishment for all three (Adam, Eve and the serpent), but He also added a promise of grace and ultimate salvation. From the very beginning God planned our rescue, and in that promise revealed some initial truths about that definitive Redeemer, Jesus.

First, it was a clear revelation of what theologians call the *"Incarnation."* The Messiah would come, somehow, in human form through the processes of natural biology, by way of a human mother. He would be human, but would be at the same time Divine, and those two natures would be perfectly manifested in one person. As one reference states it:

> The Christian doctrine of the Incarnation affirms that the eternal Son of God took flesh from His human mother and that the historical Christ is at once both fully God and fully man. It is opposed to all theories of a mere theophany or transitory appearance of God in human form, frequently met with in other religions. By contrast, it asserts an abiding union in the Person of Christ of Godhead and manhood without the integrity or permanence of either being impaired. It also assigns the beginnings of this union to a definite and known date in human history.[6]

How can we possibly understand something like that? Jesus is both human and divine, without the integrity or permanence of either being impaired? This is beyond our comprehension, and there have been many down through the ages who have denied these truths as a result. Everything that can be questioned about the proposition that Jesus Christ was one person with two natures, divine and human, has been argued.

Some have denied the deity of Christ (Ebionites, Arians). Others denied the reality of His humanity, contending that He was simply a phantom-like appearance of God (Docetists). Others declared that He was human but was adopted as divine at His baptism (Unitarians). Jehovah's Witnesses claim He was God's highest created representative, but a mere creature nevertheless. Barthians hold that He was fully human (including a sinful nature) and that God worked through this imperfect man to reveal Himself, especially at the cross.[7]

The Bible teaches, and the orthodox Christian faith affirms, that Jesus is both: born of a woman and fully human, but one with God and fully divine. This passage in Genesis, describing the creation, sin and punishment of the first humans, gives notice to this miracle of Incarnation, as mystifying as that may be to us with our limited human capacities. Dr. David Strain said it this way:

> The wonder of the Gospel is that in Christ, the infinite Son of God, the second person of the blessed Trinity, was united to human nature, to creatureliness. Without ceasing to be infinite, He entered into our finitude. Without divesting Himself of limitlessness, He embraced limits. Without ceasing to be God, He became man.

This we cannot comprehend. *Finitum non capax infinitum*—the finite cannot comprehend the infinite.[8] This mystery, one of many, we accept by faith, trusting what we cannot yet understand. Maybe someday in glory we will.

The story is told of Daniel Webster when he was in the prime of his manhood. He was dining with a company of literary men in Boston. During dinner the conversation turned to the subject of Christianity. Mr.

Webster frankly stated his belief in the divinity of Christ and his dependence upon the atonement of the Savior. Someone said to him, "Mr. Webster, can you comprehend how Christ could be both God and man?" Mr. Webster promptly replied, "No, sir, I cannot comprehend it. If I could comprehend Him, He would be no greater than I am myself. I feel that I need a superhuman Savior."[9]

That is the first truth God revealed about His Son, Jesus. He is superhuman. He is both human and divine. He became one of us as the offspring, or seed, of the woman. He lived among us, as the Gospel of John affirms:

> *"In the beginning was the Word, and the Word was with God, and the Word was God. He was with God in the beginning. Through Him all things were made; without Him nothing was made that has been made. In Him was life, and that life was the light of men … The Word became flesh and made His dwelling among us. We have seen His glory, the glory of the One and Only, Who came from the Father, full of grace and truth." (John 1:1-4 and 14)*

The second revelation concerning Jesus here in Genesis 1 is that Satan will do his best to assault, oppose, defy, resist and defeat Jesus and His work of salvation. Yes, there is a real Satan, a being of immense evil working in rebellion against God and His truth. He has labored tirelessly through the centuries to derail God's purposes and prevent God from building a people for Himself. And Satan has also toiled violently and persistently to defeat Jesus Himself.

From trying to destroy God's chosen people through whom the Messiah was to come; to trying to kill the baby Jesus once He was born (Matthew 2:16); to trying to tempt Jesus to abandon the will of God (Matthew 4:1-11); to the crucifixion itself—Satan has opposed Jesus every step of the way. He has struck at Christ's heel relentlessly, as a snake strikes at its prey, or at anyone who gets too close for its comfort.

Failing that, Satan has attacked and opposed God's people, trying to keep us from salvation by faith, trying to hinder our growth in faith and witness for the Christ—and thus defeat the purposes of God in Christ for us.

> *"Be self-controlled and alert. Your enemy the devil prowls around like a roaring lion looking for someone to devour. Resist him, standing firm in the faith, because you know that your brothers throughout the world are undergoing the same kind of sufferings."*
> (1 Peter 5:8-9)

Peter's advice is more timely and pertinent than ever. We must be on constant alert for the devices and wiles of the enemy of our souls. Now more than ever, as the great Day of the Lord draws near, the serpent will be working overtime to deceive, distract and defeat us. To deny his existence, or to underestimate his power, is a huge mistake and makes us all the more likely to fall.

In our current culture Jesus Christ—and God Himself—are being more and more openly denied, rejected and refuted. Our faith is being attacked and marginalized in shocking, blatant ways. People are working hard and speaking vehemently to erase all mention of God or Jesus in the public arena. We need to "be self-controlled and alert," resisting Satan and standing firm in our faith.

But the third revelation in Genesis 3 is great news for us, especially in the midst of that very struggle. The Messiah will come as the offspring of the woman; Satan will oppose Him at every turn; but in the end Jesus will win. Satan will strike His heel, but Jesus will crush the serpent's head. That is a statement of the enemy's ultimate, total and utter defeat. He may cause temporary chaos. He may generate great pain, heartache, sorrow and shame for us along the way. But in the end, no matter how dark and fearsome our personal lives or the world situation may seem, Jesus will crush his head.

As Revelation 17 says it:

> *"They will make war against the Lamb, but the Lamb will overcome them because He is Lord of lords and King of kings—and with Him will be His called, chosen and faithful followers."* (Revelation 17:14)

Jesus will overcome His enemies, and we with Him, along with all of His called and chosen followers. Read Revelation 19:11-21 sometime for a dramatic, stirring description of the final battle. Christ and His army of angelic warriors will strike down the nations, kings, generals and armies who oppose Him, capture the enemy and his beast, and cast them into the utter darkness of the wrath of God.

Do not allow your heart to question this or to doubt it: in the end Jesus wins. Here in the very beginning of the Bible, God's Holy and eternal Word, the end of the story is promised. A Messiah will come and through Him God will restore creation and will bring all His chosen people to eternal glory and joy in His Kingdom.

There are those who would divide God's story into separate and distinct sections. God's first attempt was to create the world and all that is in it, including the man and the woman, in order to have a people for Himself to love and with whom to share in intimate community. The first humans sinned, so God moved on to "plan B," some would say. That was to choose a nation to be His chosen people, who would live in total obedience and worship to Him and who would be a witness to all other peoples and nations of what it means to serve the one true God. But they constantly wandered from God and turned to false idols instead. That didn't work either, so the thinking goes.

So God had to come up with a "plan C." And that plan was to send His own Son, to teach people the truth, to die on the cross, to pay the penalty we deserve for our sin and to open the way for us to be reconciled to the Father.

Our text from Genesis 3 shows that Jesus was not "plan C," born of the failure of previous divine efforts to live in a loving relationship with His people. Jesus was *the plan* from day one. Jesus was *always* the plan, and everything else we may read in Scripture was the foundation leading up to His arrival on earth, or the fulfillment of it. From the very beginning, even before the fall of Adam and Eve, God was already planning His ultimate act of love, grace, mercy and redemption. Jesus was born on earth not out of frustration or desperation on God's part, but out of a grace we cannot even imagine.

This assures us that God is in loving, wise and caring control, and He always has been. He was, is and will be sovereign over all things, which gives us an unfailing sense of peace and security within, no matter how troublesome or chaotic things may be without. We can trust Him implicitly.

This also assures us of God's merciful grace. Even in the midst of His just divine punishment, He was speaking the word of grace in His promise of the Messiah, the One Who would rescue us from the dilemma of our sin. There is forgiveness for even me, the worst of sinners, to echo the Apostle Paul's words:

> *"Here is a trustworthy saying that deserves full acceptance: Christ Jesus came into the world to save sinners—of whom I am the worst." (1 Timothy 1:15)*

There is forgiveness even for you. For all who will recognize and repent of their own sinfulness, confess their need for a Savior and trust fully in who Jesus is and what He has done on the cross to atone for our sin there is the faithful, kind, gracious forgiveness of God. That is promised right here in Genesis 3. King David expressed it so marvelously in Psalm 40:1-5—

> *"I waited patiently for the LORD;*
> *He turned to me and heard my cry.*
> *He lifted me out of the slimy pit,*
> *out of the mud and mire;*
> *He set my feet on a rock*
> *and gave me a firm place to stand.*
> *He put a new song in my mouth,*
> *a hymn of praise to our God.*
> *Many will see and fear and put their trust in the LORD.*
> *Blessed is the man*
> *who makes the LORD his trust,*
> *who does not look to the proud,*
> *to those who turn aside to false gods.*
> *Many, O LORD my God,*
> *are the wonders You have done.*
> *The things You planned for us*
> *no one can recount to You;*
> *were I to speak and tell of them,*
> *they would be too many to declare."*

QUESTIONS FOR CONTEMPLATION OR CONVERSATION

1. Why do you think Adam and Eve were so easily tempted to sin by the serpent? Why was the perfection of Eden not enough for them? What else could they have possibly wanted?

2. What about you: How easily do you yield to temptations to rebel against God? What are the specific inner urges Satan uses to lure you from God's path?

3. Think about the gravity of even "small" sins. Do you think of them as "cosmic treason" or just as little and excusable errors? Why? How does that define your sense of piety and faith, and your need for a Savior?

4. How do you understand the divine/human person of Jesus? How can He be both at the same time? Do you tend to most relate to His humanity or to His deity? Why? How does your tendency in that regard influence your relationship with Him?

5. How does Jesus' ultimate victory over sin, evil, and death give you hope and comfort for the present?

CHAPTER 2

The Ruler of the Tribe of Judah

"The scepter will not depart from Judah, nor the ruler's staff from between his feet, until He comes to Whom it belongs and the obedience of the nations is His." (Genesis 49:10)

To get the full sense and context of the brief passage above, it would be well to read the whole of Genesis 49. The great Old Testament patriarch, Jacob, was nearing the end of his earthly life. He called the family together that he might speak his final words to them, particularly to his twelve sons. They were prophetic words, words of blessing to each son according to the Word of God and the result of their own lives. Jacob was speaking, but we must presume that he was under the inspiration of God's Spirit because of the oracular, predictive nature of what he said. He foretold things for each son looking far into the future, something that would have been impossible for him to do on a purely human level. At least in some measure, God Himself was speaking through Jacob.

"Then Jacob called for his sons and said: 'Gather around so I can tell you what will happen to you in days to come. Assemble and listen, sons of Jacob; listen to your father Israel.'" (Genesis 49:1)

The eldest three sons—Reuben, Simeon and Levi—received not such good news. Reuben was the firstborn and should have inherited preeminent family place and glory, but because of his sin he lost the blessings of his birth (Genesis 35:22 and 1 Chronicles 5:1-2). Simeon and Levi both were cruel and self-willed, as seen in their crime of murdering the men of Shechem (Genesis 34). Simeon's descendants were later absorbed into the tribe of Judah (Joshua 19:1), and Levi became the priestly tribe (Showing the grace of God, to be sure!) having no inheritance of their own. Simeon's numerical decline is seen when we compare Numbers 1:23 (59,300) with Numbers 26:14 (22,200).[10] I would imagine the elder three sons were just a bit disappointed, although perhaps not actually surprised given their histories.

Imagine yourself sitting in the office of an attorney as a will is being read to the gathered family. Imagine the deceased was someone close to you who was very wealthy and socially prominent. You might not like to admit it but there is some sense of anticipation and even hopefulness as the attorney reads through the last will and testament, revealing the wishes of the dearly departed for the distribution of their vast resources. After all, as a member of the immediate family, you would expect a rather nice inheritance.

But then the attorney comes to your name, and the bequest you are given is not at all as generous as you had hoped. Oh, you are to receive a somewhat reasonable portion, enough to make many envious. But it is not nearly as abundant as you had rightly—so you thought—anticipated. Naturally there would be a great letdown and a very real sense of disappointment. That must have been the scene as Reuben, Simeon and Levi sat at their father's side for their blessing.

But then Jacob came to his fourth son, Judah. He was one of Jacob's middle children. As any middle child will tell you, this is a sort of "no-man's-land" in the family hierarchy and relationships. But in this case, the birthright of the firstborn son, which Reuben had forfeited by his disobedience, fell to a middle child, Judah. As in verse 8:

> *"Judah, your brothers will praise you;*
> *your hand will be on the neck of your enemies;*
> *your father's sons will bow down to you." (Genesis 49:8)*

Judah's would be the place of honor, praise and authority in the clan. He would rule over his brothers, even those older than he, who would bow to him in submission. Judah is likened to a lion, in verse 9.

The Ruler of the Tribe of Judah

"You are a lion's cub, O Judah;
you return from the prey, my son.
Like a lion he crouches and lies down,
like a lioness—who dares to rouse him?" (Genesis 49:9)

The king of the jungle, the fiercest and most feared, but who lies down in peace, knowing he is secure. Who would dare to attack or disrupt his rest?

Judah's blessing was extensive and abundant. His future was glorious. His tribe would be the royalty of Israel from this time forward, and the scepter would not depart from them. A scepter (Hebrew *shebet*; Greek *skeptron*) is simply a staff or rod that is a symbol of rule and authority, such as denoted in Isaiah 14:5—*"The LORD has broken the rod of the wicked, the scepter of the rulers."* The symbol of the scepter was derived from the thought that a ruler was the shepherd of his people, and so at times a scepter was also used as a symbol for a ruler or shepherd.[11] This was a profoundly gracious blessing for Judah and his descendants from his father, Jacob.

Imagine being told that your family was to be royalty from this day forward. Like in a fairy tale or a made-for-TV, rags-to-riches movie, you will be the appointed and acknowledged monarch in the land, with all of the prerogatives, privileges and perquisites that entails. Yours will become a life of unbelievable wealth, honor, entitlement and power. And that throne would be handed down to your children and to their children for generations to come. News like that would be overwhelming, I'm sure, beyond anything you could have ever imagined. That may well have been what Judah was feeling at this moment, and that would have been well enough of a godsend for Judah and his descendants.

Far beyond the realm of human rule and monarchy, however, came a reference once again to the coming Messiah. The greatest windfall of all for the tribe of Judah was that the incarnated Messiah, the offspring of the woman (Genesis 3:15) would come through the lineage of Judah. The *Savior* would be a descendant of this man!

"The scepter will not depart from Judah,
nor the ruler's staff from between his feet,

*until He comes to Whom it belongs
and the obedience of the nations is His." (Genesis 49:10)*

The Hebrew there says: "He Whose it is," or "that which belongs to Him," or "Whose is the kingdom."[12] The King James Version of the Bible sought to make it even more clear—"Until Shiloh come"— capitalizing the name *Shiloh* because of the divinity of Him Whose name it is.

Shiloh was a city of Ephraim, north of Beth-el, and on the highway from Beth-el to Shechem (Judges 21:19). It was the seat of government during the time of Joshua (Joshua 21:1-2). It was the place where the tribes of Israel would often gather (Joshua 22 and Judges 21), and the home of the great prophet Eli (1 Samuel 1 and 4).[13]

But *Shiloh* is also generally understood to have been an Old Testament prophetic title for the Messiah, "The Peaceful One" as the word signifies.[14] Jacob, under divine inspiration, saw far into the future and foretold the wondrous reality that Shiloh—Messiah, Who will save us from our sins—will descend from the clan of Judah. Not only will Jesus be incarnated from the seed of a woman, but He will come through this very line.

The text above proclaims not only that He will be Messiah, but also that "the obedience of the nations" (Genesis 49:10) will be His. All the kingdoms of earth will ultimately submit to His kingship and authority, and He will rule forever. As God said it to Him in Psalm 2:

*"I will make the nations Your inheritance,
the ends of the earth Your possession.
You will rule them with an iron scepter;
You will dash them to pieces like pottery." (Psalm 2:8-9)*

He will rule over all creation with divine authority and wisdom. Can we even imagine what the world will be like to be under the governance of such a righteous, true, and fair King? One day God will exalt Jesus, the Ruler of the Tribe of Judah, to the highest place and give Him the name that is above every name, *"that at the name of Jesus every knee should bow, in heaven and on earth and under the earth, and every tongue confess that Jesus Christ is Lord, to the glory of God the Father."* (Philippians 2:9-11)

That is an amazingly encouraging assurance. Earthly human governments and rulers are just that—human. The very best of them, no matter how benevolent and altruistic, will sooner or later in some way(s) abuse the power given them and act with less than perfect motivation. Not so Jesus! His rule will be perfect and just in every way. How I look forward to that day!

That assurance, I imagine, would have struck Judah like a lightning bolt. The long-awaited Savior, the Messiah, the One for Whom the chosen people would anxiously anticipate for centuries, coming from among his very descendants! Imagine being told that one of your own grandchildren, or great-grandchildren would be the One to rescue humankind from their sins and the terrible effects of the fall. It would be an honor beyond expression or comprehension. But that is what Judah was told by Jacob, under the inspiration of God's Spirit.

And so it would indeed become reality. If we look at the lineage of Jesus recorded in the Gospel of Matthew (Matthew 1:1-17), we see that the genealogy of Christ began with Abraham, Isaac, Jacob and Judah, on down through David, all the way to Joseph. Listen to the further testimony of Holy Scripture:

Matthew 2:6—
"But you, Bethlehem, in the land of Judah,
are by no means least among the rulers of Judah;
for out of you will come a Ruler
Who will be the Shepherd of My people Israel."

Hebrews 7:14—
"For it is clear that our Lord descended from Judah, and in
regard to that tribe, Moses said nothing about priests."

Revelation 5:5—
"Then one of the elders said to me, 'Do not weep! See, the Lion of
the tribe of Judah, the Root of David, has triumphed. He is able
to open the scroll and its seven seals.'"

It's clear from all the above that our Lord Jesus did indeed descend from Judah, just as God had promised through Jacob. It is further proof of the incarnation, the fact that God came to us in human form. He had a birthplace. He had a human lineage going back fourteen generations in all from Abraham to David, fourteen more from David to the exile in Babylon, and still another fourteen generations from the exile to the Christ (Matthew 1:17).

God saw humankind in its sin, deserving of His fearful wrath. He saw the creation itself groaning under the effects of the fall. So He came to us in Jesus Christ—Emmanuel, God with us. He entered our frail existence, through the line of Judah, as one of us, in order to rescue His chosen and redeem those who will believe. For all who trust in Him there is the assurance of eternal hope and life. That was God's Word about Jesus, given through the Old Testament patriarch, Jacob.

We are not alone in a vast, cold, impersonal universe. God did not create us and then disappear from the scene, leaving us to fend for ourselves, as a deist might believe. We do not have to work our way to Him, finding some way to earn our way back into His good graces, or finding some pathway into His presence. He came into His creation as one of us, so that through faith we could one day go to spend eternity with Him. For all who believe in Christ as Savior, God is with us now in this life and will be with us forever in the glory of His eternal Kingdom.

Whatever your situation may be—no matter how isolated, marginalized, rejected, disconnected, overlooked or alone you may feel—there is Someone Who loves you and is there beside you. It is Emmanuel—God with us; God with you. You are not alone!

As this is being written, we are in the throes of the lockdown due to the Chinese corona virus. Everything is shut down, stores closed, "social distancing" the law of the land and people are self-sheltered for protection. Even churches are not supposed to gather for worship. Yes we are worshiping "together" through video, digital means, but it is not the same. We feel isolated, separated and alone; some to the point of depression or despair.

But we are not ultimately alone—ever. God is with us. The Lion of the Tribe of Judah, our Good Shepherd has come. He will never leave or forsake us. He will always hold those who love Him in the palm of His hand, to keep and protect them forever.

For thirty-eight years I was a pastor, serving as an "under-shepherd" for Christ in His church. I spoke at countless funerals over those years, and a Scripture that I used often to encourage people came from the prophet Isaiah:

> *"Fear not, for I have redeemed you;*
> *I have summoned you by name; you are Mine.*
> *When you pass through the waters, I will be with you;*
> *and when you pass through the rivers,*
> *they will not sweep over you.*
> *When you walk through the fire, you will not be burned;*
> *the flames will not set you ablaze.*
> *For I am the* Lord, *your God,*
> *the Holy One of Israel, your Savior." (Isaiah 43:1-3)*

That is God's promise (one of many) to always be with us, to uphold us and even carry us through our times of affliction and heartache. He has fulfilled it in Christ, the Seed of the Woman. When we have trusted in Christ we are His and He will not let the waters sweep over us or the fires consume us. We can trust in Him no matter what. We can rely on His presence and power to see us through. He is the Lion of the tribe of Judah.

In Bunyan's great allegory, *Pilgrim's Progress*, Christian decides to leave the Main Highway and follow another Path which seemed easier. But this Path leads him into the territory of Giant Despair who owns Doubting Castle. Eventually he is captured by Giant Despair and kept in a dungeon. He is advised to kill himself. The Giant said there was no use trying to keep on with his journey.

For the moment, it seemed as if Despair had really conquered Christian. But then Hope, Christian's companion, reminds him of previous victories. So at about midnight they began to pray, and continued in prayer until almost morning. A little before it was day, good Christian, as one half-amazed, broke out in passionate speech, "What a fool am I thus to lie in a stinking Dungeon, when I may as well be at liberty. I have a Key in my bosom called Promise that will, I am persuaded, open any lock in Doubting Castle." Then Hope replied, "That's good news. Good Brother, pluck it out of thy bosom and try." And the prison gates flew open.[15]

We have all the promises of God, many already fulfilled in Christ, some yet to come (perhaps very, very soon). We are never beyond the pale of His care or love. We can never go where He is not already there. As David poetically sang, in Psalm 139:

> *"Where can I go from Your Spirit?*
> *Where can I flee from Your presence?*
> *If I go up to the heavens, You are there;*
> *if I make my bed in the depths, You are there.*
> *If I rise on the wings of the dawn,*
> *if I settle on the far side of the sea,*
> *even there Your hand will guide me,*
> *Your right hand will hold me fast." (Psalm 139:7-10)*

This is a wonderful expression of the omnipresence of God. He is everywhere. There is *nowhere* God is not. There is no distance we can travel to take us out of His divine reach. Ask Jonah that; he of the big fish, who tried to escape God's presence but found that he could not. When the Russians sent the first cosmonauts into orbit, they came back and glibly reported that they had not seen God out there. Maybe not, but that doesn't mean He was not there. *"If I go up to the heavens, You are there."*

On the wings of the dawn, on the far side of the sea, on the heights of the highest mountain peaks, at the bottom of the deepest canyons on earth or under the sea—God is there. Even in *"the depths."* The Hebrew there is the word *"sheol."* It is the *"underworld,"* the place to which people without Christ descend at death.[16] The King James Version says it: *"If I make my bed in hell, behold, Thou art there."* (Psalm 139:8)

A shocking thought to some—that God is present even in hell! I have often heard it said, and probably said it myself along the way, that heaven is the presence of God and hell is the total absence of God. But if He is truly omnipresent then surely He is even there. He is in heaven to bless those who have trusted in His Son to save them. He is in hell to punish those who have rejected Him. There is nowhere we can go, David said, to get away from the presence of God—either to bless or to judge.

That is a sobering thought to those who refuse to bow to God through faith in the Son. But it is a priceless blessing to those who believe. Wherever we go, however far or deep, no matter what trials we face or afflictions beset us, the Ruler of the tribe of Judah will be with us. There is an ancient prayer called "St. Patrick's Breastplate." Here is part of it:

> *Christ be with me, Christ in the front,*
> *Christ in the rear, Christ within me,*
> *Christ below me, Christ above me,*
> *Christ at my right hand, Christ at my left,*
> *Christ in the fort, Christ in the Chariot seat,*
> *Christ at the helm.*[17]

❓ QUESTIONS FOR CONTEMPLATION OR CONVERSATION

1. How do you think you would feel to receive news that you and your descendants were to be royalty, with all of the prerogatives, privileges, and perquisites that entails? Would that be a good thing for you, or not? Why?

2. When have you felt terribly alone or abandoned? What was happening to make you feel so? Where did you turn for help?

3. Has God ever made His presence known to you in a time of darkness and sorrow? How did He do that? How did that make you feel?

4. What does it mean to you that God is omnipresent? Do you live with that understanding or do you tend to live as though you can sometimes hide from His presence?

5. Is God in hell? How have you understood God's omnipresence in relation to the reality and horror of hell?

CHAPTER 3

The Spirit of the Lord Will Rest on Him

"A shoot will come up from the stump of Jesse; from his roots a Branch will bear fruit. The Spirit of the Lord will rest on Him—the Spirit of wisdom and of understanding, the Spirit of counsel and of power, the Spirit of knowledge and of the fear of the Lord—and He will delight in the fear of the Lord." (Isaiah 11:1-3)

God spoke His divine word through the prophet Isaiah. The Lord sometimes spoke audibly and directly to individuals such as Moses during the great Exodus from Egypt, and the prophet Elijah in the wilderness (1 Kings 19). But often He chose to speak His words through the patriarchs and prophets, in this case Isaiah. Often the prophets would say, "Thus saith the Lord," using the old King James language, to indicate that the words to follow were not their own, but God's. (See Exodus 7:17; Joshua 24:2; Judges 6:8; 1 Samuel 10:18; and too many others to recount here.) The prophets frequently spoke the Word of God for God, at His behest, and by the direction of His Spirit.

Isaiah was wealthy by birth, well-educated and married with children. His call to the prophetic ministry was dramatic, as described in Isaiah 6, including some kind of visible manifestation of God on His throne, "high and lifted up," surrounded by seraphim worshiping God and saying over and over:

*"Holy, holy, holy is the Lord of hosts;
The whole earth is full of His glory!" (Isaiah 6:3)*

This was the time of the divided kingdom, with Israel in the north and Judah in the south. At some point in the early 700s B.C., Israel joined forces with Syria and went to war against Judah, their kin to the south. Isaiah was sent to King Ahaz with words of hope and comfort, assuring him that the Lord God would protect the nation of Judah against these aggressors. Ahaz, in keeping with his normal character and the general tone of his reign, responded with fear and unbelief, refused God's sign and sought a political solution.[18]

In the midst of God's Word to Ahaz through the prophet Isaiah, God spoke about a coming King whose rule would be markedly different from Ahaz, or any other king in the Davidic dynasty for that matter. The invading armies were described as a great forest, which God Himself would cut down (Isaiah 10:34). Even the kingly line of Judah would be cut down, and like the Assyrians there would be nothing left but stumps and the broken remains of a forest that had been totally levelled and denuded.

Sometimes as we drive through the mountains of Pennsylvania we see forests after the loggers have done their work. This is not meant as a criticism or complaint; I know progress sometimes demands lumber, and the trees are a necessary and valuable resource. Many lumber companies even have a process of replanting. But initially there often is not much left of what was previously a scenic, natural landscape. This is what God promised to do in punishing the enemies of Judah. But out of that terrible desolation, new life would arise from the ruins.

> *"A Shoot will come up from the stump of Jesse;*
> *from his roots a Branch will bear fruit." (Isaiah 11:1)*

The LORD God Almighty will cut down the mighty enemy warriors, but God's kingdom will arise, Isaiah proclaimed. The promise of God was that a tender Shoot will grow out of the stump of Jesse, David's father. Some versions call it a "Rod from the stem of Jesse," (New King James Version). The Hebrew word means a "branch," a "twig" or a "rod."[19] From the desolation of the royal house of David, this new King, the Messiah, will arise. He is Jesus Christ, the Lord.

This was a time of great national turmoil and fear in Judah. Attack was imminent and the outlook was grim. The king and the people were desperate for a word of hope from their prophet, longing for a message of encouragement to give them some glimmer of assurance in the midst of their impending national tragedy. (Like the recent worldwide pandemic, perhaps?) Instead, Isaiah looked centuries forward to their coming and ultimate hope—Messiah, the Shoot from the stump of Judah.

What an amazing description God gave to Isaiah of this coming Redeemer:

> *"The Spirit of the Lord will rest on Him—*
> *the Spirit of wisdom and of understanding,*
> *the Spirit of counsel and of power,*
> *the Spirit of knowledge and of the fear of the Lord—*
> *and He will delight in the fear of the Lord."*
> *(Isaiah 11:2-3)*

As a bit of a sidebar: This is a clear expression of the Holy Trinity, discussed briefly in the introduction. The text above is talking about *"Him"*—the coming Messiah, Jesus. But it also mentions *"the Lord"*—that's the holy name of Father God. Whenever we see that name "Lord" in all capital letters, it's the great name for God given to Moses in Exodus 3:14—YHVH, Jehovah, I AM. And *"the Spirit of the Lord"* will rest on Jesus when He comes. That's a reference to the Holy Spirit, the third person of the triune Godhead. Father, Son and Spirit are all clearly seen here in the words of the prophet, as He speaks for God.

Back to the text: The Messiah to come, promised by Isaiah and realized in Jesus Christ, will have the presence and the power of the Holy Spirit resting upon Him in a unique and commanding way. The Holy Spirit in the Old Testament would generally come upon specific individuals for certain periods of time, bestowing particular spiritual gifts as required for their calling and the task at hand.

Here we see that the Spirit of the Lord will rest on the Savior and bestow upon Him a plethora of spiritual gifts:

wisdom—He will be shrewd, prudent and astute.

understanding—He will be discerning, sensitive and discriminating of the truth.

counsel—He will give good, solid and faithful guidance.
power—He will possess mighty strength, intensity and courage.
knowledge—He will know the deep things of God and have a unique depth of perception and insight.[20]

The Holy Spirit will rest on Jesus in all of His gifts and graces. He will have the Spirit within Him—not in part but in the fullness of it, without limit. The Spirit of God shall not only come, but rest and abide upon Him. He shall have the Spirit not by careful measure but without measure, the fullness of the Godhead dwelling in Him:

"He is the image of the invisible God, the firstborn over all creation...For God was pleased to have <u>all</u> His fullness dwell in Him." (Colossians 1:15 and 19, emphasis mine)

"For in Christ <u>all the fullness</u> of the Deity lives in bodily form." (Colossians 2:9, emphasis mine)

The Greek in the latter verse speaks of the essence and the nature of the Godhead residing in Christ. "He, as man, was not merely God-like, but in the fullest sense, God."[21] The Spirit of the Father will rest upon the coming Son in such richness and completeness that He will be unlike any who has ever come before or will come after. This to the point that Jesus could honestly and legitimately say:

"Anyone who has seen Me has seen the Father. How can you say, 'Show us the Father?' Don't you believe that I am in the Father, and that the Father is in Me?" (John 14:9-10)

As we read through the New Testament we see example after example of this divine power in Christ. He taught God's truth in ways that awed and amazed His listeners. He spoke with divine authority and rare clarity. He confronted the hypocrisies, exaggerations and deceits of the religious authorities with courage and firmness. He could discern the hearts and minds of people, often responding to questions and criticisms they were afraid to even voice, perceiving their very thoughts. He healed the sick by the hundreds, granted sight to the blind, cast out demons, stilled the storm and fed hungry thousands with a small boy's brown-bag lunch.

All were clear expressions of the power of the Spirit of the Lord in the Son. They were an expression of His uniqueness and His place as the long-awaited "Shoot from the Stump of Jesse." Jesus was the One promised in Isaiah 11 and for whom Israel had waited for centuries. The long-hoped-for Branch had come!

"He will delight in the fear of the Lord." What an amazing phrase that is. Do you delight in the fear of the Lord? Do I, I wonder? What does that even mean? The Hebrew means "to delight in the odors" of something (Exodus 30:38); "smell," that is, "delight in."[22] When my wife bakes cookies, it makes the whole house smell so very pleasant, and I delight in the fragrance so much it quickly becomes very hard to resist eating one (or two, or five).

We once took a tour of a timeshare resort that we were considering investing in, and when they showed us the model condo there was someone in the kitchen baking cookies. Their job was to simply bake cookies all day long, just to make the place smell pleasant and inviting to prospective buyers. (We did buy into the timeshare, but not because of the fragrance of the cookies—at least I think not!?)

Jesus delighted not in the fragrance of cookies—well, maybe He did, in His humanity. But far beyond any such sweet smell of food, He delighted most of all in the fear of the Lord. He lived His every moment by responding to God in awe, trust, obedience and worship.[23]

One time Jesus' disciples left Him to rest at a well outside of a town in Samaria while they went into the village for food. When they returned they found Him deep in conversation with a woman who had come for water. Jesus talked to her about faith and salvation, which changed her life forever. It also transformed her village, after she told others about Jesus and brought them to Him.

When she left, the disciples urged Jesus to eat some of the food they had bought. But He said to them:

> *"I have food to eat that you know nothing about...My food is to do the will of Him who sent Me and to finish His work." (John 4:32 and 34)*

The disciples wondered if He had somehow purchased His own lunch while they were away. Maybe He had some pizzas delivered or went to a drive-thru somewhere nearby? But Jesus was saying that His very food was His delight in the will and purposes for which the Father had sent Him.

Have you ever been so immersed in a task, so focused in and concentrated on it that you lost all sense of time? You worked right through a mealtime and did not even notice or care. Hunger wasn't an issue then, only the work you were doing. That is a description of what Jesus was saying. Food—physical sustenance—took a back seat to doing what the Father sent Him to do. Speaking the Gospel into that lost woman's life was what mattered. That was what He came to do, and that was what energized and empowered Jesus.

The supreme example of this was the crucifixion itself. Jesus was so intent on doing the will of the Father, whatever that might have required, that He was willing to endure the betrayal, denials, desertions, humiliation, mockery and torture that was involved in the cross. He prayed in the Garden to be released from that horror, but added that He was more than willing to do whatever the Father asked of Him. Even then, in those horrific circumstances, it could be said that Jesus delighted in doing the will of the Father.

Which raises a question for us: What is our consuming delight in life? What is it that is the very food on which our hearts and souls exist? Is our passion focused on God and the things of His kingdom, like it was for Jesus, even if that requires of us some level of endurance, long-suffering or perseverance?

Or do we presumptuously turn that upside down and expect God to delight in doing our will? Do we demand that He provide what we think we need, give us what we think we deserve and make our lives what we desire them to be? Have we come to believe that God exists to make us happy, healthy and abundantly furnished with all that this world has to offer?

Or are there other things, or other people, we would put before Him? Jesus once said:

> *"Anyone who loves his father or mother more than Me is not worthy of Me; anyone who loves his son or daughter more than Me is not worthy of Me; and anyone who does not take his cross and follow Me is not worthy of Me." (Matthew 10:37-38)*

Those sound like rather harsh words, don't they? It may sound like Jesus was telling us to coldly set aside all familial concerns, responsibilities or connections. In fact, elsewhere Jesus stated that following Him might even cause division in families.

> *"Do you think I came to bring peace on earth? No, I tell you, but division. From now on there will be five in one family divided against each other, three against two and two against three. They will be divided, father against son and son against father, mother against daughter and daughter against mother, mother-in-law against daughter-in-law and daughter-in-law against mother-in-law." (Luke 12:51-53)*

But Jesus was making a point about priorities here. He was not suggesting that we dismiss God's call to honor and care for our parents or families, far from it. Elsewhere He chastised the Pharisees for disregarding their duty to their parents. But He was saying that as our Savior and Lord, He is to be the One to Whom we give our ultimate devotion and preference—even above our loyalty to those nearest and dearest to us.

Jonathon Edwards, 18th-century colonial American pastor and theologian, used greatly by God in the First Great Awakening, once wrote a prayer regarding his total commitment to Christ. Here is just a portion of what he prayed:

> I claim no right to myself—no right to this understanding, this will, these affections that are in me; neither do I have any right to this body or its members—no right to this tongue, to these hands, feet, ears or eyes.

> I have given myself clear away and not retained anything of my own. I have been to God this morning and told Him I have given myself wholly to Him. I have given every power, so that for the future I claim no right to myself in any respect. I have expressly promised Him, for by His grace I will not fail. I take Him as my whole portion and felicity, looking upon nothing else as any part of my happiness. His law is the constant rule of my obedience.[24]

When push comes to shove, He is to be the One to Whom we determine to give ourselves. He is to be the One we delight to honor, serve, follow and obey. He is to be the One we will cling to and refuse to deny, desert or betray. Admittedly, we all do just that more often than we even realize—we turn away from our devotion and commitment to Jesus when other pressures intervene.

How often do we refrain from offering our participation in a meaningful volunteer or ministry opportunity because there are other—more fun—things we would prefer to do with our time? How much of our time and resources do we hold as our own, rather than acknowledging our Creator God's right to maintain His Lordship over us? How many times have we turned aside from the ways of God because we have desires and plans of our own that conflicted with the moral or ethical demands of Scripture? As someone near and dear to me has always asked: "Are we giving to God the way He wants and living on the leftovers, or are we living the way we want and giving to God the leftovers?"

I have known people who have turned their backs on certain Biblical truths they once held dear (at least, I thought they did) when those teachings came into conflict with the realities of their lives. Examples abound: some accepting and affirming the divorce and remarriage of a son or daughter, when they had at one time spoken angrily against remarriage under any circumstances; others believing that homosexuality is a sin as defined by the Bible, but then totally reversing their view of that lifestyle when one of their own beloved children "comes out;" still others accepting any living arrangement their child may choose ("shacking up" was what we used to say) regardless of what God has said about proper and holy relationships between men and women; and in some cases attacking those who dared to question those sinful choices.

I understand that these matters become very difficult and quite complicated, and that parents long to—and indeed *need* to—maintain relationships with the flesh of their flesh. I agree that there are no easy answers to such dilemmas. But too often, I would suggest, we choose family over obedience to Christ in those types of situations.

> *"Anyone who loves his father or mother more than Me is not worthy of Me; anyone who loves his son or daughter more than Me is not worthy of Me." (Matthew 10:37-38)*

Jesus delighted in the will of the Father. He lived to pursue and fulfill the divine purposes of the Trinity. His consuming and defining passion was to love, serve and obey the Father. Who or what is it that fuels my life? To whom do I give my total reverence and love? To whom do I eagerly, willingly, and joyously give my ultimate subservience? That is the question we might ask ourselves in view of the example of Christ.

QUESTIONS FOR CONTEMPLATION OR CONVERSATION

1. Is there someone(s) you know on whom the Spirit of God rests in clear ways? What is it about them that makes you think that?

2. How does the Spirit of God manifest Himself in your own heart and life?

3. Do you "delight in the fear of the Lord?" How do you do so, and how does that determine your lifestyle?

4. What is the consuming passion of your life? To whom do you give your total reverence and love? To whom do you eagerly, willingly, joyously give your ultimate subservience?

5. Is there anyone or anything you hold above Christ Himself in your life priorities? What would it look like if Jesus were really number One for you?

CHAPTER 4

The Precious Cornerstone

"So this is what the Sovereign Lord says: 'See, I lay a Stone in Zion, a tested Stone, a precious Cornerstone for a sure foundation; the one who trusts will never be dismayed.'" (Isaiah 28:16)

Isaiah 28 begins a series of messages of warning from the prophet. "Woe to the crown of pride," the chapter begins, followed by an announcement of God's coming judgment on Ephraim (Isaiah 28:1-6). Ephraim was the most prominent and influential tribe of the northern kingdom of Israel, during the era when the once united nation of God's people was divided into two separate kingdoms.

A mighty and strong invading force—Assyria—was on the move nearby. Samaria, the renowned capital of Israel, reigned in luxury and pleasure, and had no fear of her enemies. They thought their fortified city was impregnable. But if these fearsome aggressors conquered the capital of the northern kingdom of Israel, then the southern kingdom of Judah would most likely quickly follow.[25] And that is exactly what Isaiah predicted, as he spoke the Word of the Lord God to His people.

Several nations banded together to resist Assyria under Sennacherib, but he quickly overwhelmed them and devastated the countryside. The northern kingdom of Israel was easily conquered and its people exiled in 722 B.C. Then Sennacherib also attacked and lay siege to Jerusalem to the south, but by God's grace the southern half of the kingdom, Judah, survived the Assyrian onslaught. Isaiah 28 through 39 detail God's message of woe through the prophet to both Israel and Judah, before any of this came to pass.

However, in the midst of these terrible "woes" comes a brief interlude of hope and assurance. The Sovereign LORD says:

> "See, I lay a Stone in Zion, a tested Stone,
> a precious Cornerstone for a sure foundation;
> the one who trusts will never be dismayed." (Isaiah 28:16)

To what exactly is God referring there? Who or what is the Stone and the precious Cornerstone? The Hebrew word for "stone" *(eben)* had many uses: charm, cornerstone, hailstone, rock, sling stone, weight and more.[26]

In this particular instance it is generally accepted that this was a reference to the coming Messiah. This was speaking of Jesus, the Son of God, to be born as the seed of the woman in the lineage of Judah. So this is God the Father speaking of Jesus the Son. And I believe He revealed two more important truths about Jesus.

First, in the Kingdom God is building, Jesus is the Cornerstone. Other translations use the word "capstone" or "keystone." These are slightly different in actual use. A *capstone* is a stone used at the top of a wall or another structure. A *keystone* is the wedge-shaped stone at the highest point of an arch that locks the others in place. I live in Pennsylvania, which calls itself the "Keystone State," and has a logo looking like that very stone at the height of an arch. A *cornerstone* is that which joins two walls where they meet at a corner.

Whichever word you choose, God is saying that His Son is the centerpiece, the foundational Rock upon which and around which the rest of His Kingdom will be constructed. Everything God will build will depend upon the Son.

> "From Judah will come the Cornerstone,
> from him the tent peg,
> from him the battle bow,
> from him every ruler." (Zechariah 10:4)

> "The Stone the builders rejected has become the Capstone;
> the LORD has done this, and it is marvelous in our eyes."
> (Psalm 118:22-24)

"Consequently, you are no longer foreigners and aliens, but fellow citizens with God's people and members of God's household, built on the foundation of the apostles and prophets, with Christ Jesus Himself as the Chief Cornerstone. In Him the whole building is joined together and rises to become a holy temple in the Lord. And in Him you too are being built together to become a dwelling in which God lives by His Spirit." (Ephesians 2:19-22).

Not only is Jesus the Cornerstone, He is the *Precious* Cornerstone. The Hebrew word speaks of something very rare, splendid and costly; something worthy of honor and admiration.[27] He is over and above any other. There is no one like Him, no one to compare.

Two gems were housed at one time in the Smithsonian Institute in Washington, D.C., under heavy guard: the Hope Diamond and the Portuguese Diamond. The Hope Diamond is considered the most beautiful blue diamond in the world. There are no words with which to describe it. The Portuguese Diamond is twice the size of the Hope Diamond and brilliantly white. When asked about the value of the jewels, a museum employee answered, "No price has ever been put on the two of them together. The Hope Diamond has been evaluated by Lloyd's of London for it was sold several times, but now it doesn't matter what the value of these two diamonds is, for they will never be sold again. They are priceless."[28] Jesus is the Precious Cornerstone infinitely more valuable than these or any other gems known to humankind.

And not only is Jesus the Precious Cornerstone, He is also the *tested* Stone. Here the reference is to something that has been carefully, meticulously examined, tried and judged, to see if it is pure and right.[29] Think of a jeweler carefully assessing a ring or pendant that someone has offered for sale, to determine its legitimacy and reasonable value. Or think of a judge cautiously and painstakingly reviewing all the pertinent evidence and testimony given to discern the guilt or innocence of the defendant. That's the sense of this word.

Surely Jesus was tested and tried as none other. Satan tempted and tried Jesus in the desert before He even began His public ministry (Luke 4:1-13), in an attempt to pull Him off course and away from His divine calling. Jesus was sorely tested by men as well. His authority was regularly questioned. His teachings were viewed with deep suspicion and scrupulously probed with complete distrust (Luke 20:1-39). His mission was totally misunderstood and misinterpreted, even by those closest to Him. He endured betrayal, denial, torture, mockery and the most painful execution ever devised. Through it all He remained obedient and faithful, even unto death on a cross (Philippians 2:5-11).

As one commentator said it, surely Jesus is "a stone of tested solidity to bear the vast superstructure of man's redemption."[30] Jesus' life of patient endurance verified the veracity of His teachings and proved Him to be the true Messiah. We can trust in Him. We can put our faith in Him and believe His work on the cross to be the sole sufficient means of our redemption. As God said it in our text, through Isaiah:

> "See, I lay a Stone in Zion, a tested Stone,
> a precious Cornerstone for a sure foundation;
> <u>the one who trusts will never be dismayed.</u>"
> (Isaiah 28:16, emphasis mine)

When we trust in Jesus we will never be dismayed. The Hebrew word means that we will never (ultimately and finally) be aghast, confounded, overwhelmed or shocked.[31] Challenges and events in this life may indeed cause us profound alarm, fear and even distress. But here we are assured that we will be secure in Him forever. Nothing will be able to separate us from the love of God in Christ:

> "For I am convinced that neither death nor life, neither angels nor demons, neither the present nor the future, nor any powers, neither height nor depth, nor anything else in all creation, will be able to separate us from the love of God that is in Christ Jesus our Lord."
> (Romans 8:38-39)

All those who come to Him in faith Jesus will hold dear, and will lose no one whom the Father has given to Him:

"And this is the will of Him who sent Me, that I shall lose none of all that He has given Me, but raise them up at the last day." (John 6:39)

We will remain totally secure in Him. Does this mean everything will be sweet and easy for us if we have faith? Some of the "health and wealth" teachers say so. They promise (wrongly) that true faith will lead to great riches and total security—in this life. And they have gotten wealthy themselves in the process. This is a false gospel.

No, trials and hardships will come to be sure, Jesus promised that much. Faith in Jesus is not a panacea to protect us from any and every difficulty. Being a follower of Christ may even be the *cause* of some of those difficulties—ask any believer who happens to live in a country that persecutes Christians. Such afflictions may someday come to these American shores too, if they have not already begun. The antagonism to our Christian faith grows more fervent every day, it seems.

But He will be with us in those hard times, holding us near and seeing us through. And those hard times may even be used by Him to refine and test our faith! Paul's sweetest epistles are from prison cells; John's divine Revelation was given to him by God and written in exile; Bunyan's classic work, *Pilgrim's Progress*, came from the Bedford jail; Luther's translation of the German Bible was completed in Wartburg Castle where he was hidden for safe keeping.[32]

Jesus is the precious and tested Cornerstone. He is worthy of His place as the foundation of God's eternal Kingdom. As the old seventh century Latin hymn says it, translated into English:

> *Christ is made the sure foundation,*
> *Christ the head and cornerstone,*
> *Chosen of the Lord and precious*
> *Binding all the church in one,*
> *Holy Zion's help forever,*
> *And her confidence alone.*

Jesus is our confidence, on which our lives are to be built. He is the only sure foundation. We can trust in Him. Jesus Himself told the little parable of the two houses. One man dug down deep and laid the foundation of his house on bedrock. When the storm came, his house stood firm because it was so well built. The other man built his house on the ground, with no firm foundation. When the storm came, his house collapsed, "and its destruction was complete." (Luke 6:48-49)

Jesus' meaning was clear. Build your life on the only truly firm foundation. There is salvation and security in no one else. "Only He [Jesus] is the basis for physical and spiritual salvation."[33] Whoever or whatever else we trust as the basis for our lives here on earth or for our ultimate standing before God will fail us. There is only one way to be reconciled with our Creator God and to be forgiven of our sins, and that is through the finished work of Christ on the cross. Don't think you can earn it or deserve it by your own merit, you can't. Trust in the Precious Cornerstone God has given—Jesus the Son.

Pliny, Roman Governor in Asia Minor in the early Second Century, was so puzzled about the Christians brought before him for trial that he wrote his famous letter to the Emperor Trajan asking for his advice.

A certain unknown Christian was once brought before him, and Pliny, finding little fault in him, proceeded to threaten him. "I will banish you," he said. "You cannot," was the reply, "for all the world is my Father's house." "Then I will slay you," said the Governor. "You cannot," answered the Christian, "for my life is hid with Christ in God." "I will take away your possessions," continued Pliny. "You cannot, for my treasure is in heaven." "I will drive you away from man and you shalt have no friend left," was the final threat. And the calm reply once more was, "You cannot, for I have an unseen Friend from Whom you are not able to separate me." What was a poor, harassed Roman Governor, with all the powers of life, death, torture and the stake at his disposal, to do with people like that?[34]

Christ, by the very Word of God, is the tested Cornerstone and the sure Foundation. This does not guarantee that we will never face hardship or persecution. But it does mean that whatever life throws at us, we will be secure in His hands and ultimately safe forever in His eternal glory. In whom or what do you trust for your security—family, wealth, position, reputation, personal abilities and intellect? It will all one day fail you. Only Christ is able to hold you and keep you, in this life and into the next.

QUESTIONS FOR CONTEMPLATION OR CONVERSATION

1. Who or what is the foundation of your life? How is this revealed in the way you daily walk through life?

2. How precious is Jesus to you? Do you think of Him as being priceless and beautiful? How does that effect how you relate to Him?

3. When in your life have you been dismayed, aghast, confounded, overwhelmed, or shocked? What was going on to make you feel that way? How did you deal with it?

4. What are you counting on to be reconciled to your Creator God? Your own goodness, your own piety, your good works in the church and elsewhere, or in Christ? Are you sure?

5. How has God used hard times in your life to test and mature you?

CHAPTER 5

My Servant, My Chosen One

"Here is My Servant, Whom I uphold, My Chosen One in Whom I delight; I will put My Spirit on Him and He will bring justice to the nations. He will not shout or cry out, or raise His voice in the streets. A bruised reed He will not break, and a smoldering wick He will not snuff out. In faithfulness He will bring forth justice; He will not falter or be discouraged till He establishes justice on earth. In His law the islands will put their hope." (Isaiah 42:1-4)

Israel's calling as the Chosen People of God was to be "a light to the nations of the world, a testament to the power and grace of God."[35] God's ultimate agenda was to bless all nations through Christ, the seed of Abraham, Isaac and Jacob. However, the history of Israel was one of continual disobedience, indifference and outright apostasy. Yes, there were sporadic renewals and revivals, but eventually God had permitted the Jews to be captured and exiled to discipline them for their sins (Isaiah 42:18-25). First the northern kingdom, then, after a time, the southern kingdom of Judah would follow suit. Jerusalem, too, would be destroyed and its people exiled.

Their captivity would not be forever. Centuries later, God would come in judgment and destroy Babylon itself (Isaiah 42:10-17). Cyrus, a pagan king of Persia, would be His servant in this matter and would allow the Jewish people to return to their Promised Land.

The prophet Isaiah therefore spoke of God's "servant" in several different ways. Israel itself was God's servant in reaching the nations for His purposes (Isaiah 41:8). King Cyrus was God's servant in restoring the Chosen People to their land (Isaiah 44:28 and 45:1). These first two were very human and fallible, prone to sin and excess.

But another, far greater Servant was coming—God's servant with a capital "S," the Chosen One. Here again, God was speaking through the prophet to talk about His Son, Jesus. God would put His Spirit upon the Chosen One, as we discussed in Chapter 3. God delighted in Him—this we will discuss later. But there are some other revelations here about Jesus for us to notice.

First of all, God makes mention here of His purpose to redeem not only the Chosen Jewish nation, but people from every nation, tribe and family of earth. Notice:

> *"Here is My Servant, Whom I uphold, My Chosen One in Whom I delight; I will put My Spirit on Him and He will bring justice <u>to the nations</u>." (Isaiah 42:1, emphasis mine)*

> *"In faithfulness He will bring forth justice; He will not falter or be discouraged till He establishes <u>justice on earth</u>. In His law <u>the islands</u> will put their hope." (Isaiah 42:4, emphasis mine)*

When the Chosen One—Jesus—comes, He will bring justice *to the nations* and on *earth* itself. The *islands* will put their hope in Him. That latter phrase calls to mind lands far from the one Promised Land, far beyond the seas, trusting in His Gospel of salvation.[36] As in Psalm 22:

> *"All the ends of the earth will remember and turn to the LORD, and all the families of the nations will bow down before Him, for dominion belongs to the LORD and He rules over the nations." (Psalm 22:27-28)*

And this is the Gospel message all the way to Revelation:

> *"Who will not fear You, O Lord, and bring glory to Your name? For You alone are holy. All nations will come and worship before You, for Your righteous acts have been revealed." (Revelation 15:4)*

God's plan and purpose all along, even as He called and worked through the Chosen People, was to redeem and call to Himself a people from among *all* races and nations on earth. That is a message of incredible grace to all of us who were not born into the race or culture of God's chosen nation. We who are Gentiles by birth (non-Jewish) can be adopted into the family of God by our faith in His Son, Jesus, and thereby become His own sons and daughters.

> *"In love He predestined us to be adopted as His sons through Jesus Christ, in accordance with His pleasure and will—to the praise of His glorious grace, which He has freely given us in the One He loves." (Ephesians 1:4-6)*

We can be grafted onto the vine, to use another Biblical image (Romans 11:17-21). Do not minimize the graciousness of that truth! You and I can be welcomed into the eternal family of God through Jesus Christ. We should never lose the wonder of that.

> *"For there is no difference between Jew and Gentile—the same Lord is Lord of all and richly blesses all who call on Him, for, everyone who calls on the name of the Lord will be saved." (Romans 10:12-13)*

The old King James Version says it: *"Whosoever believeth on Him shall not be ashamed."* And Richard Baxter, English Puritan church leader, poet and hymnist in the 1600s, once said in response:

> I thank God for that word, 'whosoever.' If God had said there was mercy for Richard Baxter, I am so vile a sinner that I would have thought He meant some other Richard Baxter; but, when He says 'whosoever,' I know that includes me, the worst of all Richard Baxters.[37]

There is hope for the worst of us. There is forgiveness even for those who think they are the best of us, because even the best of us are not good enough to earn or deserve God's mercy. Whosoever—everyone—who calls on the name of Christ can be saved unto eternal life. That is grace of unimaginable proportions. Our only response can be utter humility, reverent worship and praise. Blessed be the name of the LORD, for He has redeemed us and adopted us into His eternal family in Christ.

> *"To Him who loves us and has freed us from our sins by His blood, and has made us to be a kingdom and priests to serve His God and Father—to Him be glory and power for ever and ever! Amen."* (Revelation 1:5-6)

This fact of God's grace is what motivates and energizes our worship. Why should we get ourselves up and going every Sunday for church, when it is so tempting to snuggle in and sleep late? It is to give God the praise and reverence He deserves for adopting us into His family, to thank God for His incredible grace and to give Him glory and power for ever and ever!

This is also a call for believers to spread the Gospel around the globe. When Jesus gave His parting commission to His disciples, He said to them:

> *"But you will receive power when the Holy Spirit comes on you; and you will be My witnesses in Jerusalem, and in all Judea and Samaria, and to the ends of the earth." (Acts 1:8)*

Jesus made their (and our) purpose clear. They were to start where they were—Jerusalem, and then spread out in ever-widening circles to their state, region and the entire earth. We are to share the Good News of that adoption to all who will listen, wherever we are and wherever we go. God's salvation must be taken to the ends of the earth.

It is happening just like that. It may appear to us in the west, with our limited knowledge of or interest in the world beyond our borders, like the faith and the church are dying. They are not. There is a faithful remnant carrying on with the evangelistic call of Christ all around the world, and people are being saved every day. In his book, *Witness Essentials*, Dan Meyer lists some encouraging statistics about the growth of the church around the world:

- In 1900 Korea had no Protestant church. Today, there are over seven-thousand churches in just the city of Seoul, South Korea.
- At the end of the nineteenth century, the southern portion of Africa was only three percent Christian. Today, sixty-three percent of the population is Christian, while membership in the churches in Africa is increasing by thirty-four thousand people per day.[38]

Also:

- No Christian was officially allowed to live in *Nepal* until 1960. Now there is a church in every one of the seventy-five districts of *Nepal* with estimates of over half a million believers (*Operation World*).
- In A.D. 100, there were three-hundred-sixty non-Christians for every true believer. Today the ratio is less than seven to every believer as the *Holy Spirit* does more than we could ever ask or imagine (*Vision 2020*).
- About five hundred Muslims come to faith in Christ every month in Iran—a country ranked among the top ten persecutors of Christians in the world. Many of the new believers are young, since seventy percent of *Iran* is under the age of thirty (*Vision 2020*).[39]

So the Gospel is indeed going out to the ends of the earth. But notice *how* Jesus shared that Good News: with gentleness, kindness, compassion and firm determination.

> *"He will not shout or cry out, or raise His voice in the streets. A bruised reed He will not break, and a smoldering wick He will not snuff out. In faithfulness He will bring forth justice; He will not falter or be discouraged till He establishes justice on earth. In His law the islands will put their hope." (Isaiah 42:2-4)*

There are some wonderful word pictures in that passage. The Servant will not oppress those already beaten down and wounded by the harsh realities of life in this fallen world. A bruised reed is very fragile, easily broken and unable to stand against a harsh wind. We had some beautiful flowers come to life in the spring. They were daffodils, so I was told (No one ever accused me of being a botanist!), and they were evidently quite fragile. A spring storm blew through with heavy winds, and the next day all those pretty flowers were lying flat on the ground—like bruised reeds.

Lamp wicks were made of linen, and the allusion is to a wick that is burning with a feeble flame from lack of oil and is about to expire. The ease with which the flame of such a wick can be put out is referred to in Isaiah 43: *"and they lay there, never to rise again, extinguished, snuffed out like a wick"* (Isaiah 43:17).[40] Bruised reeds or smoldering wicks Jesus will treat with tender compassion, being careful to share God's truth in kindness and gentleness.

Have you ever felt like a bruised reed or a flickering wick, beaten down by life and battered by the winds of a fallen world? Do you even now feel worn down and tired, at the end of your rope, where just one more hurtful, damaging action against you will cause you to drop? You are not alone. There are many, I suspect, who would join you in that state of sorrow or even despair.

Jesus understands. He has experienced all the pressures, trials and temptations—and more—that we ever will. He knows what you face and how you feel. He will be gentle and compassionate with you. Matthew Henry said it so well:

> Bruised reeds, He will give them space to repent and not immediately break them; though they are very offensive, as smoking flax, yet He will bear with them, as He did with Jerusalem. Those that are weak He will be tender of; those that have but a little life, a little heat, that are weak as a reed, oppressed with doubts and fears,...He will not despise them, will not plead against them with His great power, nor lay upon them more work or more suffering than they can bear, which would break and quench them, but will graciously consider their frame.[41]

In other words, God's Chosen, Precious Servant Jesus will be patient and gentle, not overbearing, haughty or domineering. And indeed, the New Testament Gospels and the Epistles speak often of the humility and gentleness of Christ.

> "When Jesus landed and saw a large crowd, He had compassion on them, because they were like sheep without a shepherd. So He began teaching them many things." (Mark 6:34)

And the scriptures call us to treat others with whom we seek to share the faith with the same attitude. As Peter said it:

> "But in your hearts set apart Christ as Lord. Always be prepared to give an answer to everyone who asks you to give the reason for the hope that you have. But do this with gentleness and respect." (1 Peter 3:15)

In response to the fact that we have been adopted into the family of God purely by grace, there is no reason for us to be proud or self-righteous. In view of the example and life of Christ, there is no room for haughtiness, arrogance or self-aggrandizement in our hearts.

In our relationships with those who have not yet bowed before God in repentance and faith in Christ, perhaps the best attitude should be, as the saying goes: "There but for the grace of God go I." Yes, we want to speak the Word of God into the lives of others along the way, but we want to do so thoughtfully, carefully, considering their situation and needs. It will do them—or us—no good to come across in an intimidating, condescending, or patronizing way.

Christ treated people with respect and care. So should we, and we should do so with great patience and forbearance. Our text assures us that Jesus will not weaken or be disheartened until God's purposes are fulfilled. Neither should we. I have known Christians, perhaps you have as well, who were sincere believers and who truly cared about the salvation of others around them. But they approached the task of reaching out to them in an overbearing, demanding, forceful and even condescending manner that actually turned people away and gave them cause to reject the claims of Christ. I shudder to think that I may have sometimes done so myself!

Please do not hear this as an excuse to never speak about Christ to family, friends, classmates or coworkers. Many of us do that too little already. Statistics show that most believers (at least in the west) have never led anyone to faith in Christ—not even one! We need no further rationale to excuse our disinclination and reluctance to address spiritual matters with those near and dear. But this may be a call to do so with gentleness and kindness, not as a "bull in a china shop."

> *"Therefore, as God's chosen people, holy and dearly loved, clothe yourselves with compassion, kindness, humility, gentleness and patience. Bear with each other and forgive whatever grievances you may have against one another. Forgive as the Lord forgave you."* (Colossians 3:12-13)

It is said that when Mrs. Booth (wife of the founder of the Salvation Army) was a little girl, running along the road with hoop and stick, she saw a prisoner dragged away by a constable to the lockup. A mob was hooting at the unfortunate culprit, and his utter loneliness appealed at once to her heart. It seemed to her that he had not a friend in the world. Quick as wink she sprang to his side and marched down the street with him, determined that he should know that there was one soul that felt for him whether he suffered for his own fault or that of another.[42]

Perhaps that illustrates what we are saying here. Jesus came to this earth to walk by our side, to die for our sins and to gently and kindly draw us home to God. Our job, as saved and forgiven believers, is to gently walk beside others and to draw them in as well.

QUESTIONS FOR CONTEMPLATION OR CONVERSATION

1. How have you experienced the gentle, caring presence of Christ in the hard times of your life? How did He provide kind help and comfort?

2. What in life makes or has made you feel like a fragile reed or a flickering wick? When have you felt especially weak and vulnerable? Who or what held you up and saw you through?

3. How comfortable are you in speaking to others about Christ? Do you easily speak about spiritual matters or is that something that comes hard for you? Why do we hesitate so?

4. Has anyone ever "come on too strong" with you in trying to witness to you, speak Christ into your life, or call you to deeper maturity? Have you ever done so with others?

5. Have you ever led/helped anyone to make a faith commitment to Christ? If not, why not: is it because you are embarrassed or afraid to try, or simply because God has never allowed you to experience that joy? If so, how did it make you feel to be so used by God?

6. How have you contributed to the spread of the Gospel in your community and in the world? What more could you do in that regard?

CHAPTER 6

Called and Kept

*"This is what God the L*ORD *says—He Who created the heavens and stretched them out, Who spread out the earth and all that comes out of it, Who gives breath to its people, and life to those who walk on it: 'I, the L*ORD*, have called You in righteousness; I will take hold of Your hand. I will keep You and will make You to be a covenant for the people and a light for the Gentiles, to open eyes that are blind, to free captives from prison and to release from the dungeon those who sit in darkness.'" (Isaiah 42:5-7)*

In our last chapter, we looked at God's Word about His Son, Jesus, through the prophet Isaiah. Specifically we studied verses 1 through 4. In this chapter, we will go back to Isaiah 42, beginning with verse 5. Something quite extraordinary happened there. God the Father stopped speaking *about* Jesus, the Son, and began to speak *to* Him! As one commentator said it, "Previously God had spoken of Messiah; now (Isaiah 42:5-7) He speaks to Him."[43]

We are privileged here to be given a glimpse into the inner workings of the divine Trinity, as one Person of the Triune Godhead speaks to another. We are allowed to eavesdrop on the intimate conversations within God Himself, as the plan of the ages for our salvation is discussed. How amazing is that? And the Father said some wonderful things to the Son, as follows.

"I, the LORD, have called You in righteousness."

The Hebrew word *qara*, means "to call," "to proclaim," or "to summon."[44] God *chose* Jesus for this task. Was it a command, a demand or a mandate? In its various ancient uses the word could mean any of the above. In the New Testament, Jesus prayed to the Father:

> *"I have brought You glory on earth by completing the work You gave Me to do."* (John 17:4)

The Greek in that case means "to assign a person a task for the benefit of others," and to "appoint."[45] This was the Son's appointed task within the purposes of God for humankind and for His creation.

But the sense that we get from Scripture as a whole is that it was a mutual agreement among the Father, Son and Spirit. It was the unified plan from before the beginning of time. He was called *"in righteousness."* This means Jesus was appointed to fulfill God's righteous, just and merciful plan. Because of our sin we deserve His wrath and judgment. Because of His grace, His eternal and righteous plan from before the beginning of time was for the Son to pay the penalty we deserve on the cross.

This was not something foisted or forced upon the Son against His will. Yes, He was called to it, but He accepted it willingly and chose to go to the cross for our salvation. He could have walked away at any time. He could have said, "No way am I going to suffer and die for these sinful, disobedient scoundrels and scalawags! I'm out of here!" He could have called down the angel armies to protect Him from the soldiers. He could have simply come down off the cross as those who mocked Him scornfully challenged Him to do.

Instead, He willingly took it upon Himself to fulfill the eternal purposes of God for our benefit.

> *"And being found in appearance as a man, He humbled Himself and became obedient to death—even death on a cross."* (Philippians 2:8)

> *"Let us fix our eyes on Jesus, the Author and Perfecter of our faith, who for the joy set before Him endured the cross, scorning its shame, and sat down at the right hand of the throne of God."* (Hebrews 12:2)

He humbled Himself. He did that of His own free volition. He freely chose the joy and the glory set before Him from before the creation of the world in order to finish the work of salvation. For that we owe Him our undying praise, adoration and obedience. We need to now live for Him Who gave Himself for us:

"And He died for all, that those who live should no longer live for themselves but for Him who died for them and was raised again."
(2 Corinthians 5:15)

To be totally honest, I don't know if I can say that I no longer live for myself, or that I now *fully* (or even *mostly*?) live for Him who died for me. I would *like* for that to be true, but I strongly suspect there is too much of me and not enough of Him in my viewfinder. Hall of Fame football player Gale Sayers used to say, "The Lord is first, my friends are second, I am third." I wish I could be so focused. How about you?

"I will take hold of Your hand. I will keep You."

The second thing the Father said to the Son was an assurance of His constant care and protection. The Father will take hold of the Son's hand to keep Him. The word means to "watch," "guard" or "protect."[46] The clear sense is that though the Father called the Son to a very difficult task, He would be with Jesus through it all, holding His hand, so to speak, to preserve and sustain Him all along the way.

And all through the time of Christ's earthly ministry, God (almost) never left Him or forsook Him. God was there with Him, to empower and protect. At the very beginning of His ministry, in His hometown of Nazareth, the people were skeptical. They eventually became offended by His teachings. Furious, they got up, drove Him out of the town, and took Him to the brow of the hill on which the town was built, in order to throw Him down the cliff. But He walked right through the crowd and went on His way (Luke 4:16-30).

Another time, in Jerusalem, at the time of the Feast of Dedication, Jesus was in the temple area walking in Solomon's Colonnade. A crowd of

Jews gathered around Him and asked Him point blank if He was the Christ. When He plainly said yes, they picked up stones to stone Him. But when they tried to seize Him, Jesus simply walked away (John 10:22-39).

Now how do you suppose He did that? Only by the care and protection of the Father was Jesus able to simply walk through a violent mob intent on murder, with no harm coming to Him. Only by the strength of God was Jesus able to heal the sick, raise the dead, cast out demons and still the storm. God was with Him all the way, that much is clearly evident.

However, there was one dramatic exception—when Jesus was on the cross. When all the sins of the world were laid upon Him, the Father turned away. In what must have been for Jesus the most heart-rending, painful and shocking aspect of the whole horrifying crucifixion, for the first time in all eternity the Father abandoned the Son. And Jesus cried out,

> "*Eloi, Eloi, lama sabachthani?*"—*which means*, "*My God, My God, why have You forsaken Me?*" *(Matthew 27:46)*

This was a direct quotation from Psalm 22:1. It was on the cross that Jesus, who was sinless, was made "to be sin for us" (2 Corinthians 5:21). He had been forsaken by the Father! He became "a curse for us" (Galatians 3:13). This has to do with the holiness of God. How could a pure and perfectly holy God look with favor on His Son who had become sin?[47] God turned from the sin that Christ carried to the cross. Can we even imagine how painful that must have been for the Son, Who had lived with the Father through all eternity past in perfect intimacy and loving communion? It is beyond our comprehension.

I think of people we have known who had been married for fifty, sixty, some even seventy years. Even at my most compassionate, I cannot begin to imagine the heartache and loss felt by the survivor when their partner of that many years has died. Losing the one with whom you had enjoyed six or seven decades of joy and intimacy is unimaginable. Some have described it as having lost the best part of their own self.

So how can we even imagine or express the pain Jesus must have felt to have the Father turn away from Him on the cross? We can't. But that was the exception. That was a temporary, though horrifying situation. Other than that, God the Father held, kept, guided and guarded the Son without fail.

Amazingly, He has promised to be with us, too. As Moses said to the people of Israel:

"Be strong and courageous. Do not be afraid or terrified because of them, for the Lord your God goes with you; He will never leave you nor forsake you." (Deuteronomy 31:6)

As Jesus said it in the Gospel of John:

"I will not leave you as orphans; I will come to you." (John 14:18)

We will not be friendless, without associates who may be of sustaining help.[48] Jesus will hold and keep us just as surely as the Father held and kept Him, of that we can be certain; because Jesus promised it.

When journalist James Gordon Bennett sent Henry M. Stanley to search for David Livingstone in Africa, he said: "Draw on me for a thousand pounds today to provide your equipment, and when that is exhausted, draw on me for another thousand, and when that is done, draw another; but find Livingstone."

God authorizes us to draw on Him. As the Chosen People wandered through the wilderness on the way to the Promised Land, God fed them with a daily portion of manna from heaven. Each day He gave them just enough for that day, then again the next, and the next. It was always there and it never ran out.

When one day's supply is exhausted, we are to draw another and then another, and then another.[49] His supply will never run out. He will always be there for those who are His, and we can trust Him no matter what.

"I will…make You to be a covenant for the people and a light for the Gentiles, to open eyes that are blind, to free captives from prison and to release from the dungeon those who sit in darkness."

This third message is describing the amazing ministry to which God had called the Son. It was global. It was expanded beyond the Chosen People, the Jews, to include the Gentiles and all who would believe (see previous chapter). Remember what Jesus said in His hometown before the people rose to throw Him out of town?

> *"The Spirit of the Lord is on Me, because He has anointed Me to preach good news to the poor. He has sent Me to proclaim freedom for the prisoners and recovery of sight for the blind, to release the oppressed, to proclaim the year of the Lord's favor." (Luke 4:18-19)*

Jesus was simply repeating God's calling given to Him in Isaiah 42. This is what He was called to do and what He passionately gave Himself to accomplish.

And this is the mission in which we are called to participate. We are privileged to be welcomed to share in the eternal work of the Son in reaching the peoples of the world with the Good News of His Gospel. How we do that is an individual matter.

I was a pastor for thirty-eight years, and my wife and I were blessed to witness and even participate in the saving and sanctifying work of Christ in the people of those four congregations. But not everyone is called to be a pastor.

> *"It was He who gave some to be apostles, some to be prophets, some to be evangelists, and some to be pastors and teachers, to prepare God's people for works of service, so that the body of Christ may be built up." (Ephesians 4:11-12)*

> *"And in the church God has appointed first of all apostles, second prophets, third teachers, then workers of miracles, also those having gifts of healing, those able to help others, those with gifts of administration, and those speaking in different kinds of tongues. Are all apostles? Are all prophets? Are all teachers? Do all work miracles? Do all have gifts of healing? Do all speak in tongues? Do all interpret? But eagerly desire the greater gifts." (1 Corinthians 12:28-31)*

How has God gifted you? What can you do to contribute to the building of God's Kingdom on earth? In small ways and large, in public and in private, in leading and in serving, in endless manners and matters, we can enlist in the purposes of God.

In an interview a businessman was asked, "How many employees work here?" He replied, "Very few!" He had many employees on the payroll; it was just that few of them actually did any real work. If someone asked that question about your church, what would the reply be? In many cases the "precious few" carry the load.[50] It's because so few are willing to contribute to and participate in the ministry of the church.

After a revival service at which Dwight L. Moody spoke, a cultured lady criticized Moody for his poor use of grammar. And it was most likely true—he was not the most erudite or cultured of orators. He used plain language that was not always grammatically correct. The evangelist replied, "You seem to use grammar well enough. What are you doing with it for the Lord?"[51] His point being that whatever gifts or abilities God had given him, he was using them for Kingdom purposes. And she should be doing the same.

An interesting event from the Gospel of Matthew illustrates this well. After a long day of teaching and healing, Jesus went to Peter's house for a night of rest. Upon arrival, He discovered that Peter's mother-in-law was ill with some kind of fever. Dr. William Barclay suggests that it was most likely malaria, which was common in that particular region.[52] In any case, she was not at all well. Jesus simply touched her hand, and she was healed. As soon as the fever left her, she rose and began to wait on Him (Matthew 8:14-15). He healed her, and her response was to immediately begin to serve Him in the best way she knew how, using the abilities she had been given.

A much more dramatic example could be found in Isaiah 6. There the prophet is given a vision—his only one, whereas some other prophets were given many[53]—of the Lord seated on a throne, high and exalted, and the train of His robe filled the temple. This was the Lord Jesus, judging by the title Adonai, and according to John 12:41. In response to the glory and majesty of the divine Christ, Isaiah is overwhelmed with the sense of his own sin, and cried out:

> *"Woe to me! I am ruined! For I am a man of unclean lips, and I live among a people of unclean lips, and my eyes have seen the King, the L*ORD* Almighty."*

A heavenly seraph was sent to touch his lips with a hot coal from the altar and to take away the guilt of Isaiah's sin. He was forgiven! And then he heard the voice of the Lord saying, *"Whom shall I send? And who will go for Us?"* And Isaiah immediately cried, *"Here am I. Send me!"* (Isaiah 6:1-8)

After being forgiven and cleansed of his sin, Isaiah was eager to do something tangible to express his profound gratitude, and quickly volunteered to go and do whatever Christ needed of him. He didn't even know where he would be sent or what he would be asked to do when he got there. But he was anxious to give himself to the purposes of the Lord.

What about me? What about you? We who have been healed in the deepest sense possible—forgiven by the grace of God of our deep and heinous sin and restored to righteousness in Christ—how are we responding to what He has done for us? In gratefulness to His overwhelming love to us, how are we expressing our gratitude to Him, and are we doing so in tangible ways? Are we using whatever abilities God has given us for Kingdom purposes? Pray the God of the universe to show you what you can do—and get busy!

QUESTIONS FOR CONTEMPLATION OR CONVERSATION

1. How does it make you feel about Jesus that He would willingly accept God's call to come to earth as our Savior, and to die on the cross for our sin? How can we respond to that knowledge?

2. How does it make you feel that the God of the universe would welcome you to be a partner in His eternal purposes? What does that say about God? What does that say about you?

3. How has God gifted you? Are you using whatever abilities God has given you for Kingdom purposes?

4. In gratefulness to His overwhelming love to you, how are you expressing your gratitude to Him, and are you doing so in tangible ways?

CHAPTER 7

The Lord Our Righteousness

*"'The days are coming,' declares the L*ORD*, 'when I will raise up to David a righteous Branch, a King who will reign wisely and do what is just and right in the land. In His days Judah will be saved and Israel will live in safety. This is the name by which He will be called: The L*ORD *Our Righteousness.'" (Jeremiah 23:5-6)*

We jump ahead—in time and in Scripture—to the prophet Jeremiah. Jeremiah ministered as a prophet from sometime around 640 B.C. to 586 B.C. He spoke warnings from God to the nation of Judah of coming judgment for their disobedience, and lived to see his prophecies fulfilled through two separate invasions by King Nebuchadnezzar of Babylon. He was a faithful voice for God, unpopular because of his messages of doom, and his life was in peril more than once.

In the midst of stern warnings of His coming wrath, God spoke through the prophet an astonishing word of hope and salvation, quoted above. But to fully understand that encouraging word, we must put it into context.

Jeremiah 23 begins with stern words for the leaders—"shepherds"—of Judah. Those who were supposed to protect and care for the people were in fact ruthlessly oppressing and abusing them. As Warren Wiersbe states it:

> Instead of *leading* the flock in love, they *drove* it mercilessly and exploited it. The shepherds didn't visit ("care for") the sheep, but God would visit the leaders with punishment. Because the leaders disobeyed the Law and refused to trust God, they destroyed the nation and scattered the flock among the Gentiles.[54]

The prophet Ezekiel was even more harsh and direct:

"The word of the LORD came to me: 'Son of man, prophesy against the shepherds of Israel; prophesy and say to them: This is what the Sovereign LORD says: Woe to the shepherds of Israel who only take care of themselves! Should not shepherds take care of the flock? You eat the curds, clothe yourselves with the wool and slaughter the choice animals, but you do not take care of the flock. You have not strengthened the weak or healed the sick or bound up the injured. You have not brought back the strays or searched for the lost. You have ruled them harshly and brutally. So they were scattered because there was no shepherd, and when they were scattered they became food for all the wild animals.'" (Ezekiel 34:1-5)

The leaders of the nation and even the priests and religious authorities, who were called to care for God's people, were caring only for themselves. In the process they actually caused great harm to those they were called to shepherd.

There are those in the church still today who are supposed to be caring for the flock under them but who are caring only for themselves. The New Testament speaks often of wolves in sheep's clothing within the body, which are doing great damage (Matthew 7:15-20). There have always been those who have claimed to be called by God to ministry, but who are there much more so for their own personal reasons of gaining prestige or imposing "on the generosity of local congregations to live a life of comfortable, even pampered, idleness."[55] Fortunately the vast majority of pastors and priests are people of integrity and true calling, and they sincerely care about and for their people. But there are a few others who use their position for their own personal, emotional and even financial ends.

Back in my seminary days I knew a few students who seemed to be studying and seeking ordination not out of any real sense of calling from God, but rather to make a stand for personal rights and to be a part of what they considered to be a necessary sexual and gender revolution within the church. I cringed to think of the harm they would cause once they actually got their hands on a local congregation.

This is also a continuing issue with some of the political leaders of our own great nation. Thankfully not all—there are good, faithful politicians who care deeply for this nation and seek to serve their constituents with great integrity. However, there are also those who use their positions of influence not to shepherd or care for their citizenries, but to build up their own bases of power and financially enrich themselves.

Over the years I have seen some of our United States senators become very, very wealthy during their time in office. And I have wondered: How did they amass so much wealth on a senator's salary? How is it that some of our elected officials enter their term of office with minimal financial resources but leave some years later with wealth beyond imagination? They certainly aren't paid that much. They have used their position to enrich themselves, sometimes by unethical and even illegal means.

That's why the founders of our republic were very intentional about carefully including a series of checks and balances in the formulation of our constitutional government. They had a healthy and realistic perception of the sinfulness of those who lead and the temptations they would encounter to abuse their power.

The same was true in the time of the prophet Jeremiah. The chapter begins with harsh words of condemnation directed at the sin of the so-called shepherds and leaders of the people, who were taking them into ruin.

However, God said, *"The days are coming when I will raise up a righteous King who will rule with wisdom, justice and compassion."* He will be a shepherd of the people in the best and fullest sense of that word. He will do what is right in the land and under His leadership the people will live in security and prosperity.

In His realm, Judah, the southern kingdom, and Israel, the northern half of the divided nation, will be reunited and live together under this one righteous King. That was a clear eschatological (end times), Messianic reference, as in Jeremiah's day the Jews were centuries away from anything resembling political or religious union.

This righteous King being referenced here was the Messiah—Jesus. God the Father was speaking once again about His beloved Son, Jesus. And He gave us a name by which the Son should be known: *"The Lord Our Righteousness"* (Jeremiah 23:6). That phrase is significant, and we must consider it carefully.

We should notice, first of all, that God the Father called Jesus *"The Lord."* In your version of the Bible that name will most likely be spelled with all capital letters. Even if it is not so written in your particular translation, in the original Hebrew this was the sacred, proper name for the God of Israel. This is the personal, revered name of God reflected in the tetragrammaton, YHWH (יהוה, yhwh); meant to convey the eternality, self-existence, and changelessness that belong to God alone.[56]

But here God gave that same divine name to be used of Jesus! That is a profound, crucial truth about the Son. Once again we see reference to the Trinity. The Son is one with the Father. *Both* are Lord God, Yahweh. Both are referred to with the incomprehensible, incommunicable divine name.[57] God Himself was speaking of the Son and giving Him this sacred, unique name. The divinity of Christ is at issue here and is clearly confirmed by the words of God Himself.

Jesus used this same sacred name to refer to Himself on several occasions. The Greek form was *egō eimi* (ἐγώ εἰμί). Sometimes Jesus used this phrase to simply describe Himself in metaphorical terms, especially in the Gospel of John: "I am the bread of life" (6:35); "I am the light of the world" (8:12); "I am the door" (10:7); "I am the good shepherd" (10:11); "I am the resurrection and the life" (11:25); "I am the way, and the truth, and the life" (14:6); "I am the true vine" (15:1). In these many cases the use of the phrase could be said to have simply been common human language in the first person.

In other instances, however, Jesus used this phrase in the absolute, divine sense where it clearly referred to God. In using the expression, Jesus seemed to be explicitly identifying Himself with Yahweh, asserting His eternality, self-existence and changelessness, and claiming to be Yahweh's presence on Earth.

In passages where Jesus made an "I Am" statement in this sense, the negative reaction of His opponents reinforces the view that the phrase amounted to a claim to deity. For example, John 18:6 records that those who came to arrest Jesus "drew back and fell to the ground" when He identified Himself with the words "I Am." When Jesus described Himself as "I Am" in John 8:58 the Jews attempted to stone Him because they interpreted His words as a blasphemous claim to deity.[58]

In short, here in Jeremiah 23 God Himself identified Jesus by using the sacred name "Yahweh," and Jesus Himself on several occasions claimed that name for Himself. Jesus is one and the same with the Father, Yahweh God.

It is crucial for us to understand that Jesus is divine, because *"only as God could His life, ministry and redeeming death have infinite value and satisfy the demands"*[59] of God's holiness. In other words, only as a sinless human could Jesus truly die for others. But only as holy God could His death truly save us. Here God Himself clearly confirmed that Jesus is God, a theme repeated by John's Gospel:

> *"In the beginning was the Word, and the Word was with God, and the Word was God. He was with God in the beginning." (John 1:1-2)*

The Son of God, Jesus, Messiah, was God Himself in human form, and His ultimate kingdom will one day come, bringing a restoration of the fallen world and a peace and prosperity we can hardly imagine. Whereas some of the shepherds of God's people before Him (and since) were corrupt, deceitful and selfish, the Father promised to send a Ruler Who will truly care for His people. Jesus claimed for Himself the title of the Good Shepherd (John 10:1-18), saying that He is the Promised One of God, who will protect, provide and even die for His sheep. The Gospels show the truth of this in abundance.

But the righteousness mentioned here is referring not only to a political justice, national security or even world peace. It is infinitely more than any earthly domain, however benevolent, though a new and recreated heaven and earth will ultimately be a part of it.

The Messiah will not simply bring righteous governance to earth, but He will *be* our righteousness before God. He will be *"The Lord Our Righteousness."* (Jeremiah 23:6) As Paul said it in 1 Corinthians:

> *"It is because of Him that you are in Christ Jesus, who has become for us wisdom from God—that is, our righteousness, holiness and redemption." (1 Corinthians 1:30)*

He will not only be righteous and just Himself, as our Shepherd, He will be *our righteousness.*

The word "righteousness" in the verse above refers literally to the act of doing what God requires or doing what is right.[60] But the same word is a term that has to do with our standing before God. God declares us righteous by grace, through our faith in Jesus Christ.

By ourselves, we can never be good enough or do enough good and pure deeds to counter balance our sin. *"There is no one righteous, not even one; there is no one who understands, no one who seeks God. All have turned away, they have together become worthless; there is no one who does good, not even one."* (Romans 3:10-12) There is no one righteous before God—not one. Not even me. Not even you. However pious, good and pure we may think we are, we do not deserve God's forgiveness.

All those who are predestined and set apart to belong to God and to serve Him are by faith set free from our sin and death because, and only because, Jesus Christ paid the price for us on the cross.[61] We are forgiven and saved only by the grace of God (*sola gratia*), only by the sacrifice of Christ on our behalf (*sola Christos*), and only through our faith in Him (*sola fide*).

When the Spirit of God enables that saving faith within us, God counts Jesus' righteousness as ours. God sees not our sinfulness but Christ's sinless perfection, and counts us as pure and forgiven. We have a phrase that refers to seeing the world "through rose-tinted glasses." It means that we perceive the world around us by looking at things in an optimistic, positive way. We see things through the perspective of our optimism. God looks at His own through the lens of Christ's obedience and perfection. He sees not us, in that sense, but Jesus.

In theological terms God *imputes* Christ's righteousness to us. Christ is perfect and righteous, we are not. But God counts His righteousness as our own, when we put our faith in Jesus. God puts Jesus' righteousness on our account, in place of the debit of our sin. It is not the believer's own righteousness (or lack thereof) that God sees when He looks at us, but Jesus' righteousness deposited into our account. We are welcomed into the family of God—by grace through faith in Jesus. Therefore, in a very real sense, Jesus *is* our Righteousness, exactly as God said it through the prophet Jeremiah.

In Jeremiah 23 and beyond, God promised that a faithful, godly remnant of His people would return to their land after the many years of exile. But God promised an even greater gathering that would occur when the Messiah comes. Through Jesus, God would begin to build His kingdom on earth, and when Jesus returns in the last days of human history (at the end of this present era) that eternal kingdom will be consummated fully.

The Jews in exile during the days of Jeremiah were encouraged by the promise of His coming. How much more can we who believe in Jesus be encouraged by the promise of His ultimate victory and reign as King of kings and Lord of lords? The Greek philosopher Socrates once cried out: "Oh, that someone would arise, man or god, to show us God."[62] Someone did—His name is Jesus, "The Lord Our Righteousness."

Our response is to humbly and gratefully bow before Jesus and accept the righteousness He offers us, and to put aside any arrogant pretension that we can ever deserve it on our own account. We must put on the pure white robes of His righteousness and lay aside the filthy rags of our own sinfulness, if we ever hope to come into the presence of a holy God.

Some years ago—quite a few, actually—I played on our high school basketball team. The coach had a dress code for "away" games that he strictly enforced, because, as he said, we were representing our school wherever we went and needed to do so with some sense of propriety and class. For some strange reason, one time I showed up for the bus wearing a rather casual outfit. It was not at all what the coach had made clear that he expected. The coach took one look at me and said, "You're not getting on this bus looking like that!" Fortunately, I had arrived early enough that I had time to hurry home and change into something more appropriate. I have ever since respected that man for holding firm to his standards.

There's a dress code for us, too. Jesus offers to clothe and cover us with His righteousness, and thereby make us fit for the presence of the Father. If we ignore that and try to enter wearing the clothes of our own goodness, we will "not be allowed on the bus." It is only when we accept Jesus as our Righteousness that we are properly clothed and prepared to humbly and gratefully, with awe and reverence, bow before the throne of the King.

QUESTIONS FOR CONTEMPLATION OR CONVERSATION

1. Have you enjoyed the ministry of a faithful "shepherd" in your lifetime, someone who served God and therefore you with integrity and authentic faith? Be sure to thank them and continue to pray for them!

2. How have you faithfully served others as a "shepherd" or caretaker? To whom could you do so now?

3. Do you think of Jesus as equal to God the Father, as also the great I AM? If so, how does that awareness manifest itself in your daily life? If not, what might it look like for you to begin to relate to Him on those terms?

4. What are you counting on for your standing before God? Who or what is your righteousness, honestly?

5. Do you truly realize that you are God's child only by grace through faith in Jesus? How does that affect your relationship with God?

CHAPTER 8

The Sovereign Son of Man

"In my vision at night I looked, and there before me was one like a Son of Man, coming with the clouds of heaven. He approached the Ancient of Days and was led into His presence. He was given authority, glory and sovereign power; all peoples, nations and men of every language worshiped Him. His dominion is an everlasting dominion that will not pass away, and His kingdom is one that will never be destroyed." (Daniel 7:13-14)

As we read through the Old Testament book of Daniel, we see that the first six chapters tell the personal history of Daniel. Those chapters include three beloved and iconic stories: the four Hebrew boys being taken to Babylon and tested in the king's court; the fiery furnace; and the lions' den. If those stories are not familiar to you, now would be a great time to read them! Daniel and his friends stood firm in their faith and were ultimately vindicated. Along the way, Daniel rose in the king's court and became a high official in the Babylonian government. Part of that rise in authority was driven by Daniel's God-given ability to interpret dreams.

The most dramatic instance of this was in Daniel 2, where King Nebuchadnezzar had a terrifying dream. He demanded his priests and seers to interpret it, but he refused to tell them what the dream was. They begged him to tell them the dream so they could interpret it for him, but he refused and threatened to kill them all if they failed to tell him what it meant. Daniel heard of this grave situation, and went to the king, offering to give him the information he needed.

The Sovereign Son of Man

After a night of prayer with his friends, Hananiah, Mishael and Azariah (Shadrach, Meshach, and Abednego were their Hebrew names), God granted Daniel the grace to know and interpret the king's dream. In response, the king placed Daniel in a high position of authority in the kingdom and lavished many gifts on him. He made him ruler over the entire province of Babylon and placed him in charge of all its wise men (Daniel 2:1-49).

But now we turn to Daniel 7. Until now, Daniel had been interpreting the dreams of others. Now God gave him a series of extraordinary visions of his own.[63] This one began with great winds churning the waters of the sea, and four strange, magnificent beasts arising from the waves: a lion with the wings of an eagle; a bear holding three ribs in its mouth between its teeth; a leopard with four wings like those of a bird, and with four heads; and a fourth beast—*"terrifying and frightening and very powerful. It had large iron teeth; it crushed and devoured its victims and trampled underfoot whatever was left. It was different from all the former beasts, and it had ten horns."* (Daniel 7:4-7) Those who study and write about the events at the end of human history have had a field day trying to interpret and explain this vision of the four beasts, and what they might portend as related to current and future world events. I will not presume to do so, nor is that our focus here.

Our focus is on what follows, at verse 13 and 14. There God gave Daniel a much more glorious vision, in my opinion—a vision of Jesus. As we contemplate the things God has said about Jesus, this one must be included in our study.

> *"In my vision at night I looked, and there before me was one like a Son of Man, coming with the clouds of heaven." (Daniel 7:13)*

Daniel was given a revelation of heaven itself, and in that vision is shown *"one like a Son of Man"* approaching the Ancient of Days (Jehovah God) and being led into His presence. This is Christ: the Offspring of the Woman, the Ruler of the Tribe of Judah, the Precious Cornerstone, the Chosen Servant, called and kept by God, and our Righteousness. What we see here is God the Father and God the Son, together, in the throne room of heaven.

And here He is given the name "Son of Man." Some scholars suggest that the phrase "Son of Man" is either a title for the people of Israel considered corporately or for their angelic representative in the heavenly court.[64] But given the description that follows, I believe it is—here at least—clearly a designation that refers to Jesus.

It was, after all, Jesus' favorite title for Himself, used often in the Gospels. It was how Jesus most often referred to Himself during His earthly ministry.[65] See: Matthew 8:20; Matthew 9:6; John 1:51; John 3:13; and many others. In fact, with only a few exceptions, the title was used only by Jesus and rarely by anyone else, perhaps as a humble way of referring to Himself simply as a human being.[66]

Perhaps Jesus was trying to emphasize that He came as one of us. Jesus came to save humans. This meant that He had to take on Himself flesh and blood and become a Man. Only then could He die and through His death defeat Satan.[67]

> *"Since the children have flesh and blood, He too shared in their humanity so that by His death He might destroy him who holds the power of death—that is, the devil—and free those who all their lives were held in slavery by their fear of death...For this reason He had to be made like His brothers in every way, in order that He might become a merciful and faithful high priest in service to God, and that He might make atonement for the sins of the people." (Hebrews 2:14-17)*

The title Son of Man, of which Jesus was so fond, shows that He identified with our humanity. He shared our common lot and conquered sin and death on our behalf. God gave Jesus that name, and He embraced it willingly and fully. And because He did so, God gave the Son sovereign authority over all creation.

> *"He was given authority, glory and sovereign power; all peoples, nations and men of every language worshiped Him." (Daniel 7:14)*

Even before Jesus died, rose, and ascended to heaven, He was given full authority and sovereignty over all peoples and nations. That eternal reign had already begun, but it will not be consummated until Jesus returns.

When He comes again, and God puts all of His enemies under Him, Jesus will then finally and fully rule as sovereign King.

The Apostle Paul described all this with profound, poetic reverence in one of my favorite passages in all of Scripture:

> *"Who [Jesus], being in very nature God,*
> *did not consider equality with God something to be grasped,*
> *but made Himself nothing,*
> *taking the very nature of a servant,*
> *being made in human likeness.*
> *And being found in appearance as a man,*
> *He humbled Himself and became obedient to death—*
> *even death on a cross!*
> *Therefore God exalted Him to the highest place*
> *and gave Him the name that is above every name,*
> *that at the name of Jesus every knee should bow,*
> *in heaven and on earth and under the earth,*
> *and every tongue confess that Jesus Christ is Lord,*
> *to the glory of God the Father." (Philippians 2:6-11)*

And therein must lay our only proper response to this wondrous Son of Man, Jesus. It is to bow on our knees in total awe and praise, confessing Jesus as Lord and Savior, to the glory of God the Father, Who called and sent Him in the first place. One day every knee will bow to Him and every tongue on earth will confess Him as Lord. Those who have trusted Him will bow in worship. Those who have refused His offer of salvation and rejected Him will fall on their faces in abject terror at His just judgment and wrath. Either way, we will all bow to Him.

The call here, going back as far as the days of the prophet Daniel in the Old Testament, is to kneel before Him now, accepting His salvation for ourselves and submitting to His authority over us in this life and in the eternity to come. The famed psychiatrist, Dr. Carl Jung of Switzerland, once said that in thirty-five years of counseling people with personal problems, none of them had gotten right with themselves until first they got right with God.[68]

How does one "get right with God?" Not by works, not by their own goodness or piety, not through church attendance or giving. It is only by grace, through faith in Jesus. We need to humbly kneel before the Son of Man and submit to His sovereign authority.

Ty Cobb was a Hall of Fame major league baseball player. He played more than three thousand games and twelve times led the American League in batting average. For four of those years, he batted over .400, an unheard of and unmatched feat. He was also widely known as a hard-drinking, coarse, degenerate scoundrel. He lived hard and he played baseball even harder. He was a feared baserunner because he seemed to relish the opportunity to injure other players with his spikes, some say sharpened for that purpose. There is good reason to believe that he killed a man in a bar fight. He had few friends.

In his dying days he accepted Jesus Christ as his Savior. He said, *"You tell the boys I'm sorry it was the last part of the ninth that I came to know Christ. I wish it had taken place in the first half of the first."*[69] How different his life and legacy might have been if he had not waited until the last days to kneel before Christ. My call here (and indeed, God's call) is for us to make sure we don't do the same. The challenge for us is to bow before the Son of Man *now*, repenting of our sin and turning to Him for our salvation. There is no other way.

And one more thing God said about His Son, through the prophet Daniel. His kingdom will have no end! All earthly kingdoms eventually come to an end. None lasts forever. Sometimes a great power overtakes them. Often they crumble from within, overcome with their own decadence and recklessness. Many have claimed an endless rule—none have succeeded.

Nationally syndicated columnist and political commentator Cal Thomas (a favorite of mine and many others) recently wrote a book titled *America's Expiration Date: The Fall of Empires and Superpowers . . . and the Future of the United States*. In this powerful and prophetic book, Mr. Thomas offered a diagnosis of what exactly is wrong with the United States by drawing parallels to once-great empires and nations that declined into oblivion. Citing the historically proven two hundred and fifty year pattern of how superpowers rise and fall, he predicted that America's expiration date is just around the corner and shows us how to escape their fate.[70]

We here in the United States are on the same course that all other world powers have taken. All began well, declined and ended ingloriously. None were forever. Even America will not last indefinitely. Mr. Thomas, and many others, believe that the decline has begun already. The only debate seems to be whether or not it is too late to stem the tide and change that trajectory. Jesus' kingdom alone is eternal. It will have no end.

> *"Your throne, O God, will last for ever and ever;*
> *a scepter of justice will be the scepter of Your kingdom."*
> *(Psalm 45:6)*

And those who have bowed before Him as Savior and Lord will enjoy that eternity in glory with Him. That is the ultimate hope and joy that sustains us even when things on this earth look bleak. Life in this fallen world may be cruel at times. It may be very, very hard. But there is an infinite, ultimate joy that awaits us that will far outweigh anything we have endured here.

Hebrews 11 addresses this very theme quite dramatically. It reminds us of many of the great heroes of the faith: Abraham, Isaac, Jacob, Joseph, Moses, Joshua, Rahab and many others, who accomplished remarkable things with God and for His purposes by faith. They *"through faith conquered kingdoms, administered justice, and gained what was promised; who shut the mouths of lions, quenched the fury of flames and escaped the edge of the sword,"* (Hebrews 11:33-34), and much more. Theirs were stories to celebrate.

But Hebrews 11 also acknowledges many others, nameless thousands, who for the sake of their faith were tortured, faced jeers and flogging, were chained and put in prison, were stoned, sawed in two and put to death by the sword. They were destitute, persecuted and mistreated. They lived by faith, too, and refused to surrender their hope in God, but never saw in this life the rewards of that trust.

> *"All these people were still living by faith when they died. They did not receive the things promised; they only saw them and welcomed them from a distance. And they admitted that they were aliens and strangers on earth. People who say such things show that they are*

looking for a country of their own. If they had been thinking of the country they had left, they would have had opportunity to return. Instead, they were longing for a better country—a heavenly one. Therefore God is not ashamed to be called their God, for He has prepared a city for them." (Hebrews 11:13-16)

"These were all commended for their faith, yet none of them received what had been promised. God had planned something better for us so that only together with us would they be made perfect." (Hebrews 11:39-40)

Our trust in Christ and in our ultimate, eternal glory with Him is what enables us to carry on no matter what we face here and now. We know that someday, perhaps soon, we will be with Him in the splendor of the new earth and all will be well. Armed with that assurance we stand strong in hope. As Paul said it so well:

"Therefore we do not lose heart. Though outwardly we are wasting away, yet inwardly we are being renewed day by day. For our light and momentary troubles are achieving for us an eternal glory that far outweighs them all. So we fix our eyes not on what is seen, but on what is unseen. For what is seen is temporary, but what is unseen is eternal." (2 Corinthians 4:16-18)

During World War II, German pastor and theologian Dietrich Bonhoeffer was imprisoned by the Nazis for his stand against the German regime, and for his part in a plan to assassinate Hitler. On Sunday, April 8, 1945, Pastor Bonhoeffer held a little worship service, which reached the hearts of all his fellow captives. He had hardly finished his prayer, when the prison door opened. Two evil-looking soldiers came in and barked: "Prisoner Bonhoeffer, come with us!" The words meant only one thing—the scaffold. He had been condemned to be executed, and this was the assigned day. As he bid his fellow prisoners goodbye, he said, "For me this is the beginning of a new life, eternal life."[71]

I do not know what dangers, trials or afflictions you must deal with this day. Nor do I wish to minimize them in any way. I understand that life in this fallen world can be hard and harsh. It has been for me at times, too; though maybe not to the level of yours. But I do know this. Jesus is Lord. He is sovereign over all peoples and nations. He is even now building His kingdom, and will one day come back to fulfill and consummate it. His kingdom will have no end, and those who have trusted in Him will live forever with Him in the glory of His eternal presence.

QUESTIONS FOR CONTEMPLATION OR CONVERSATION

1. Do you think God still speaks to people through dreams? Why or why not? Has He ever spoken to you in a dream?

2. How do you understand the title "Son of Man," in reference to Jesus? What does that say to you about Him?

3. What does it mean to you that Jesus came from heaven to be "one of us?" How does that encourage or comfort you?

4. In what ways, literally and figuratively, do you bow on your knees in awe and praise to Jesus as Lord and Savior?

5. As you look at the state of affairs in our nation and in the world at large, what feelings rise up within you? Hope? Fear? Dread? Sorrow? Why?

6. How does your ultimate and eternal victory in Christ help you cope?

CHAPTER 9

The Source of Our Peace

"Therefore Israel will be abandoned until the time when she who is in labor gives birth and the rest of His brothers return to join the Israelites. He will stand and shepherd His flock in the strength of the LORD, *in the majesty of the name of the* LORD *His God. And they will live securely, for then His greatness will reach to the ends of the earth. And He will be their peace." (Micah 5:3-5)*

In the throes of the American Civil War (1863), poet Henry Wadsworth Longfellow wrote some verse that was set to music and became a beloved Christmas carol. Longfellow wrote about the angelic choir that appeared to the shepherds in the field, praising God and saying:

"Glory to God in the highest, and on earth peace to men on whom His favor rests." (Luke 2:14)

In response, the poet wrote:

> *I heard the bells on Christmas day*
> *Their old familiar carols play,*
> *And wild and sweet the words repeat*
> *Of peace on earth, good will to men.*

But then Longfellow looked out at the carnage across the land as the war raged on. By the time it ended, 650,000 to 1,000,000 soldiers and civilians were dead; another 750,000 or more were wounded and maimed; countless homes, businesses, and farms utterly destroyed. Considering the ongoing bloodshed and destruction all around him, Longfellow's mood turned melancholy, and he wrote:

> *And in despair I bowed my head*
> *"There is no peace on earth" I said,*
> *"For hate is strong and mocks the song*
> *Of peace on earth, good will to men."*

Many today, looking at the violence and chaos in our contemporary world, would agree with his despondency and hopelessness in that moment. Read the newspaper, or check your favorite site in the digital media; though it's true that we must use wise discretion in choosing our source of news—not everything we hear or read out there is fair or accurate! Nevertheless, certainly still today there is no peace on earth—at least in any political or nationalistic sense, or in our current era of cultural upheaval and contention.

The poem did end, however, with a note of great assurance and hope as he proclaimed:

> *Yet pealed the bells more loud and clear*
> *"God is not dead, nor doth He sleep,*
> *The wrong shall fail, the right prevail,*
> *With peace on earth, good will to men."*

It is a song of great hope and joy, even in the face of terrible wrong. From where does that kind of assurance come? How can one find peace on earth when earth is a place of warfare, danger and peril? In this chapter we will look at a passage in the Bible in which God tells us the answer to that very question. Our peace—our only real and lasting peace—will come from His Son, the Messiah, Jesus.

The Old Testament prophet Micah brought a message of terrible judgment against God's people. In Micah 1 he spoke of God's judgment against both Samaria—capital city of the northern kingdom of Israel—and Jerusalem—capital city of the southern kingdom of Judah. He went on to directly name twelve cities and pointed out their specific sins against God. All had rebelled against God and rejected His sovereign authority over them. All had fallen into idol worship, carving statues and bowing before them. In all these cities and more, fraud, violence, oppression, abuse of the poor and rulers who did not obey God's Law were the norm.

Does any of that sound familiar? Our culture looks quite the same in many respects. We worship idols of every type, things made by our own hands. Violence, fraud, oppression and leaders who have turned their backs on God are all hallmarks of our contemporary society. Could God's judgment be as near for us as Micah warned it was for God's people in those ancient days? I for one believe it quite probable.

This was a message of woe that brought Micah no joy. He had no pleasure in bringing it to the nation of his birth and to his own people. He wept in deep lament and grief:

> *"Because of this I will weep and wail;*
> *I will go about barefoot and naked.*
> *I will howl like a jackal*
> *and moan like an owl." (Micah 1:8)*

How I too grieve and mourn for our nation as it walks further and further away from the God of our founders. How sad it is to see our culture abandon the godly heritage on which it was built. How depressing it is to see so many not only turn away from God but actually become aggressively antagonistic to anything that even hints of the one true faith. How frightening it is to consider the coming judgment of God that seems inevitable given how far we have strayed from Him.

Nevertheless, in Micah 5 the tone of the whole message suddenly shifted. In the midst of these great woes and laments, God gave His prophet a word of great hope. A new Ruler is coming, God promised. Yes, Micah 5:3 says that Israel will be abandoned by God—for a time; but not forever.

Micah had earlier mentioned those twelve cities that were singled out for direct punishment, a dubious distinction. But now in 5:2 he named one more. This one—Bethlehem Ephrathah—is lifted up for remarkable honor. Bethlehem will be the birthplace of the Messiah, as promised to Judah centuries before.

"She who is in labor," the scripture says (Micah 5:3, NIV). In the older King James version it reads, *"Until the time that she which travaileth hath brought forth."* Who is she who "travaileth" in labor? Scholars see this as a reference to the virgin mother of the Messiah.[72] Isaiah, fellow prophet and Micah's contemporary, used similar language:

> *"Therefore the Lord Himself shall give you a sign; Behold, a virgin shall conceive, and bear a Son, and shall call His name Immanuel." (Isaiah 7:14)*

God's promise was that through the virgin, One will come who will restore God's kingdom. He will shepherd His flock in the fullest sense of that term. He will stand in the strength and the majesty of the name of the LORD His God. His people will live securely and His greatness will reach to the ends of the earth. The day will come when Mt. Zion will become the capital of the world; all the armies will be dismissed and the weapons destroyed. It will be a glorious time of reunification, rebirth, and rebuilding of the kingdom of God's people.[73]

"And the rest of His brothers return to join the Israelites." (Micah 5:3) This is most likely, in one sense, a reference to the Jewish nation, the remnant of which will someday be returned to their Promised Land and their hearts turned back to their covenant with God. One day under the rule of the true Shepherd "the Jewish nation shall return to the spirit of the true genuine children of Israel, a people in covenant with God; the hearts of the children shall be turned to the fathers."[74]

But many scholars have seen this also as a promise to all who would become the true children of Abraham through their faith in Jesus, the Shepherd Savior. When He comes to consummate His kingdom we too will enjoy the glorious, eternal kingdom of God's people, living in the security of His presence and in faithful covenant with our heavenly God. That is our assurance as well, as believers in Christ.

Even beyond that eventual, eternal hope, ("Pie in the sky, by and by," some have derisively called it.) we can have the hope and assurance of Christ for today, because as God said it through the prophet: *"And He will be their peace."* (Micah 5:5)

Longfellow bemoaned the lack of peace in his day. The same could be said for most every day of human history before or since. I have no way of checking or confirming this, but I suspect it is at least close to being accurate—it has been said that only eight percent of the time since the beginning of recorded history has the world been entirely at peace. In over 3,100 years, only 286 have been warless and 8,000 treaties have been broken in this time.[75]

In the political sense, there will be abiding peace only when Christ returns and makes all things new. At that point, finally and fully, the dwelling of God will be with us and He will live with us. We will be His people and God Himself will be with us and be our God. *"He will wipe every tear from [our] eyes. There will be no more death or mourning or crying or pain, for the old order of things has passed away."* (Revelation 21:4)

Until then, as God promised, He—Jesus—will be our peace. In wartime and in pandemics, in poverty and in need, in oppression and in persecution, He is our peace.

He is our peace with God. As Paul stated it in Ephesians 2:

"Remember that at that time you were separate from Christ, excluded from citizenship in Israel and foreigners to the covenants of the promise, without hope and without God in the world. But now in Christ Jesus you who once were far away have been brought near through the blood of Christ. For He Himself is our peace..." *(Ephesians 2:11-14)*

Also in Colossians:

"For God was pleased to have all His fullness dwell in Him [Jesus], and through Him to reconcile to Himself all things, whether things on earth or things in heaven, by making peace through His blood, shed on the cross." (Colossians 1:19-20)

Jesus is our peace with God. Before Jesus we were separated from God by our sin nature and our sinful lives, foreigners and aliens, without hope and without God. We were in fact at war with God and under His wrath (Colossians 1:21), enemies of the Father and in adamant rebellion against His sovereign authority. In Jesus we are reconciled to our Creator, brought near by the blood of His cross and made children of the heavenly Father. He is our peace with God.

The once mighty Napoleon is reported to have made this statement:

> Alexander, Caesar, Charlemagne and myself founded empires; but on what foundation did we rest the creatures of our genius? Upon force. But Jesus Christ founded an empire upon love; and at this hour, millions of persons would die for Him. I die before my time, and my body will be given back to the earth to become food for the worms. Such is the fate of him who has been called the 'great Napoleon.' What an abyss between my deep misery and the eternal kingdom of Christ, which is proclaimed, loved, adored and is still existing over the whole earth.[76]

He is our peace within. Apart from Christ we are lost in sin, shame and guilt. We may not acknowledge that fact, or even be aware of it most days. We may try to solve that problem through a variety of tactics and attempts. We may try to drown those feelings in drink or drugs. We may try to raise our own self-image by comparing ourselves to others we judge to be lesser. We may try to counter the guilt by being the best person we can possibly be. We may try to achieve some great thing (like write a book?) to prove to ourselves (and others) that we really are very good people.

But underneath it all, there is an awareness (conscious or otherwise) that we are not who or what we ought to be. We do not measure up. We are not the exemplary human beings we like to think ourselves to be.

Jesus is our peace within. Jesus fully recognized our sin and shame. He acknowledged that we are not the people God created us to be. He knows that as sinners separated from God we deserve only judgment and wrath.

He did not dismiss or minimize our predicament. He took our sin to the cross and paid the penalty we deserve! He provided for the possibility that we might be reconciled to God by our faith in Him.

The path to peace within is not to deny, ignore or try to hide our sinfulness. It is to admit and acknowledge our wrong attitudes and behaviors to ourselves and to God, turn away from those sins and replace them with godly actions and words, trusting in Jesus and the righteousness He gives us (see Chapter 7) and placing ourselves in His hands. He is the One who brings us near to God and provides the way for us to be brought into the family of God.

He is also our peace of mind and heart in a second way. Our faith gives us a sense of calm and security within no matter what is going on around us. In situations of utter turmoil, hardship, uncertainty and even danger, we can rest in His presence and care. Jesus said:

> *"Peace I leave with you; My peace I give you. I do not give to you as the world gives. Do not let your hearts be troubled and do not be afraid." (John 14:27)*

The world gives a peace based on circumstances. If you "have all your ducks in a row," if all your relationships are copacetic, if you have enough money, food, and material comforts, if you are safe from any and all outer perils, then you can have peace within. But if there are any stressors in these or any other facets of your life, then that tenuous worldly peace abruptly disappears.

Jesus offers a peace within based on the assurance of His presence and care, on the promise of our forgiveness and reconciliation with God and on our ultimate home with Him in the kingdom of God. As the Prophet Isaiah said it so profoundly:

> *"The fruit of righteousness will be peace; the effect of righteousness will be quietness and confidence forever." (Isaiah 32:17)*

Jesus is our peace within.

He is our peace with one another. Once we have peace with God and have been reconciled to our Creator, once we have been given the peace of Christ in our own hearts, we can then and only then have some semblance of peace with others. Only then can we put aside our own egos, our own narcissistic self-focus, our own perceived rights and privileges and love others as we have been loved (and as we already love ourselves!). Calls to sincerely love others abound in scripture—John 13:34-35:

> *"A new command I give you: Love one another. As I have loved you, so you must love one another. By this all men will know that you are My disciples, if you love one another."*

> Romans 12:9-10: *"Love must be sincere. Hate what is evil; cling to what is good. Be devoted to one another in brotherly love. Honor one another above yourselves."*

> 1 Peter 1:22: *"Now that you have purified yourselves by obeying the truth so that you have sincere love for your brothers, love one another deeply, from the heart."*

> 1 John 3:11: *"This is the message you heard from the beginning: We should love one another."*

It is impossible for us to fully love others unless we have the love of God within us through faith in Christ. We can then love them with His love, not through our own meager measure. We can love them as He has loved us. We can forgive them as He has forgiven us. We can put aside our prejudices, distrust, and fear of others to simply love them as those beloved by God. As someone wisely said it:

> Christian love rises above human differences to show itself in absolute loyalty to others in their need. Christian love looks on other persons through the eyes and with the heart of God. Christian love respects others as persons who are objects of God's love.[77]

Jesus is our peace with one another. Of course, the world at large has rejected the Prince of Peace, so there has been no peace in the world. But when Christ returns to earth, He will establish His kingdom of peace and there shall be no more war.[78]

> *"He will judge between the nations*
> *and will settle disputes for many peoples.*
> *They will beat their swords into plowshares*
> *and their spears into pruning hooks.*
> *Nation will not take up sword against nation,*
> *nor will they train for war anymore.*
> *Come, O house of Jacob,*
> *let us walk in the light of the LORD." (Isaiah 2:4-5)*

That glorious day of peace is coming! Meanwhile, we can have peace in our hearts—with God, within ourselves, and with others—by trusting Christ as Savior, and living in submission to His Spirit and Word. It is this prophecy in Micah 5 that led the wise men to Jesus. May it lead us to Him as well!

❓ QUESTIONS FOR CONTEMPLATION OR CONVERSATION

1. As you look at the violence and chaos in our contemporary world, would you agree with Longfellow's despondency and hopelessness, or with his hopefulness and assurance? Why?

2. How has Jesus given you peace with God? Within your own heart and soul? With others?

3. Is it hard for you to love others as God has loved you? What makes that so difficult for many of us?

4. What are some ways we could begin to show Christ-like love to others? To whom could you do so today?

5. Do you live with a daily anticipation of the eternal peace Christ will one day—perhaps soon—bring to His people and His creation? How does that affect your life?

CHAPTER 10

The Beloved Son of God

"Then Jesus came from Galilee to the Jordan to be baptized by John. But John tried to deter Him, saying, 'I need to be baptized by You, and do You come to me?' Jesus replied, 'Let it be so now; it is proper for us to do this to fulfill all righteousness.' Then John consented. As soon as Jesus was baptized, He went up out of the water. At that moment heaven was opened, and He saw the Spirit of God descending like a dove and lighting on Him. And a voice from heaven said, 'This is My Son, Whom I love; with Him I am well pleased.'" (Matthew 3:13-17)

We move now to the days of the New Testament. For over 400 years, the nation of Israel had not heard the voice of a prophet. The silence was deafening, at least to those few who were faithfully seeking and serving the LORD.

Then John the Baptist appeared and a great revival took place. John's preaching centered on repentance and the kingdom of heaven. To *repent* means "to change one's mind and act on that change." John was not satisfied with regret or remorse; he wanted "fruits meet for repentance" (Matthew 3:8). There had to be evidence of a changed mind and a changed life. All kinds of people came to hear John preach and to watch the great baptismal services he conducted.[79] "The whole Judean countryside and all the people of Jerusalem went out to him." (Mark 1:5) Tax collectors, soldiers, even Pharisees and Sadducees came to him. Many confessed their sins, and were baptized by him in the Jordan River.

Surprisingly, one of those who came to John for baptism was Jesus. But Jesus was sinless, and needed no such repentance or change of heart and life. He was the one and only perfectly pure human being.

> *"For we do not have a high priest who is unable to sympathize with our weaknesses, but we have One who has been tempted in every way, just as we are—yet was without sin." (Hebrews 4:15)*

So why did Jesus go to John to be baptized? Even John himself hesitated, and said, *"I need to be baptized by You, and do You come to me?"* But Jesus replied, *"Let it be so now; it is proper for us to do this to fulfill all righteousness."* (Matthew 3:13-15)

Jesus was not baptized because He was a repentant sinner, so many reasons have been suggested:

- to give approval to John's ministry;
- to consecrate His own coming ministry;
- to allow John to give an official introduction of Jesus to the Jewish nation;
- to anticipate Jesus' baptism of suffering on the cross;
- to allow Jesus to identify with the sinners and publicans He came *to save*.

Jesus Himself talked about insisting on His baptism to "fulfill all righteousness." Matthew Henry understands that in terms of the propriety and gracefulness in everything that Christ did for us. That is, Jesus did this to "own every divine institution, and to show His readiness to comply with all God's righteous precepts." Thus Christ fulfilled the righteousness of the ceremonial law and at the same time recommended the sacrament of baptism to His church for future generations of believers.[80]

However we understand Jesus' reasoning, He insisted on being baptized by John, and after some serious hesitation John conceded and took Jesus with him into the water. And it was after John baptized Jesus that God spoke in a clear and audible way.

First, God the Holy Spirit descended like a dove and alighted on Jesus. Whether this was in the form of a real, physical dove, or in some kind of vision—Jesus saw it, John saw it, and many presume that the bystanders saw it as well. With the symbol of a peaceful and gentle bird, Jesus was empowered by the Spirit for His coming ministry and work of salvation.

And then, God the Father verbally spoke to God the Son, for all to hear:

"This is My Son, Whom I love; with Him I am well pleased." (Matthew 3:17)

A quick sidebar before we move on: yet again we have a clear manifestation of the Holy Trinity. We see God the Father, Spirit and Son all involved in this sacred baptism and all clearly evident. He is God in three Persons, blessed Trinity. Over and over in Scripture we see clear expressions of the triune God.

Now we look at what the Father said to and about the Son. I would suggest three things in particular:

"*This is My Son*" That is an expression of relationship. Jesus Christ is the eternal Son of God. We discussed earlier the title which Jesus often gave Himself—Son of Man, humbly identifying Himself with humanity as a whole. Here God identified Jesus with Himself, the divine, eternal and sovereign ruler of all creation. As the angel messenger said it to the virgin, Mary:

"The Holy Spirit will come upon you, and the power of the Most High will overshadow you. So the Holy One to be born will be called the Son of God." (Luke 1:35)

By God's own testimony, Jesus is the Son of God. Except for once in the Gospel of John (John 10:36), Jesus did not call Himself "Son of God." But His common use of "Father" ("Abba") in addressing God (Matthew 11:25-26; Mark 14:36), which was unique in Jewish prayer; and His claim of special knowledge of God as Father; imply that special relationship.[81]

Some, like the Jehovah's Witnesses, have interpreted this to mean that Jesus is not divine, but a being created by God. They would say that the creedal phrase "only begotten Son of God" implies that Jesus is simply a created human being, special in some senses, but not God Himself. This title is sometimes referred to as proof that there is but one God—Jehovah, Yahweh, God the Father—and that the whole doctrine of the Trinity is false.

But as the Apostle John said it in his Gospel:

"For God so loved the world, that He gave His only begotten Son, that whosoever believeth in Him should not perish, but have everlasting life." (John 3:16, King James Version)

The word *"begotten"* is the Greek *"monogenes."* According to most scholars, this is not a reference to creation or conception but rather "to what is unique in the sense of being the only one of the same kind or class—'unique, only.'"[82] Others translate it as "unparalleled," or "incomparable."[83] Hence the more modern New International Version translates that verse by saying that God gave "His one and only Son." This is much closer to the meaning of the sentence.

Jesus is God, the second Person of the Trinity, since before the beginning of time. Jesus was not created by God, He was *with* God in the beginning, and He *was* God all along (John 1:1). Here the voice of the Father from heaven confirms and affirms the unique, sacred relationship Jesus had and still has within the eternal, divine Godhead.

"Whom I Love" In the King James Version the phrasing is: *"This is my beloved Son."* "Beloved" is a word rich in meaning. It refers to one who is the only one of his or her class, but at the same time is particularly loved and cherished—'only, only dear.'"[84] In other words, God said, in essence, "This is My one and only dearest Son, Whom I love as no other."

Jesus was with God through all eternity, living with Him in utter oneness and love. The Father, Son, and Spirit shared in infinite personal intimacy, with no hint of division or discord. We can't even imagine a relationship that pure, that full, or that perfect. But that is the love with which the Father loves the Son. Jesus is God's beloved.

Think of your love for your child, simply because they are flesh of your flesh, aside from anything they say or do. They are your child. From the moment of their birth, from the moment of their conception, maybe even from the moment they were a thought and hope in your mind, you have loved them. They are "the apple of your eye." They are your cherished and treasured one, above all other children on earth.

There is a story that is told in 1 Kings of the Old Testament to illustrate the wisdom of Solomon. It also expresses the love of a parent for their child. Two prostitutes, living in the same house, each gave birth to a child within the space of a few days. The baby of the one woman died, and in her grief she switched the babies and claimed the living child as her own. The actual mother of that living child, of course, protested, and they took their dispute to the king for a resolution.

After explaining what had happened, and after both mothers insisted that the living child was their own, King Solomon said:

"This one says, 'My son is alive and your son is dead,' while that one says, 'No! Your son is dead and mine is alive.'…Bring me a sword." (1 Kings 3:23-24)

So they brought a sword for the king, and he ordered them to cut the living child in two and give half to one and half to the other. Immediately the child's true mother cried out and begged the king to give her son to the other woman, rather than to kill him. She put her son's life ahead of her own heart's need for him. Solomon instantly knew which woman was the true mother (1 Kings 3:16-27).

I think of a second example, in the Old Testament book of 2 Samuel. Chapter 15 and following chronicle the revolt of David's son, Absalom, as he staged a coup against his own father, swept into power, and drove David into exile. Civil war resulted, David's men eventually were victorious, and Absalom was killed. When David heard the news, it is recorded that the king was deeply distressed:

"The king was shaken. He went up to the room over the gateway and wept. As he went, he said: 'O my son Absalom! My son, my son

Absalom! If only I had died instead of you—O Absalom, my son, my son!'" (2 Samuel 18:33)

This was the son who had rebelled against David and driven him from his throne, in disobedience to God. And yet, when he was killed and David was restored to power, rather than rejoice at the military victory of his men of valor, David wept inconsolably for his insubordinate son. In fact, David's general, Joab, went in to the king and scolded him for humiliating the warriors who had just saved his life and restored to him the throne.

The love of a parent for their child is just like that. A parent will sacrifice their own happiness for their beloved child. A parent will do whatever is in their power to provide for and protect their beloved child. A parent will give their own life for the flesh of their flesh. Multiply that many times over (infinitely?) and you have a glimpse of the affection and devotion of God for Jesus.

And this is not to even mention the love the Father must have felt for the Son because of His willingness to take on the burden of the cross in order to pay the penalty for our sins. Imagine a child of yours achieving some great task. Think of the pride, joy and depth of feeling you might experience as a result. That might be a minute fraction of the love God felt for the Son because of His suffering and death. Jesus consented to the eternal plan of salvation, delighted to do the will of the Father, no matter how hard and harsh, and agreed to suffer and die for those who were lost. Surely God's love for Jesus must have swelled and deepened because He laid down His life for His sheep. Surely Jesus was the *beloved* Son of God.

"With Him I Am Well Pleased" The Father was *well pleased* with the Son. God "took pleasure in" the Son. He was "delighted with" the Son. He was "glad in Him." It's the same word Isaiah used to describe God's gracious pleasure in His people as His own beloved possession (Isaiah 62:4). A way to paraphrase this would be to think of God as saying, "This is My one and only dear Son; I am very pleased with Him."[85]

It was a word of great affirmation, of deep commendation and approval. Jesus pleased the Father in giving up the glory of heaven to be incarnated as the God-Man. As we have already seen above, the Father was pleased with His willingness to give Himself for our salvation. But this was spoken even before Jesus walked to the cross and suffered such horrific pain and degradation! God was *already* well-pleased with the Son. It was not a conditional thing, given only because of what Jesus did. It was because of who Jesus was and is.

That raises a profound question for us. Do we love and adore Jesus only because of what He does for us and gives to us? Is our worship conditional and dependent on blessings received? Does our veneration of Him wane when things don't go as planned and life becomes hard? Do we become disappointed and even angry with Him when He does not answer our prayers when we want, in the ways we demand?

Or do we bow before Him in praise simply for who He is, apart from anything that He has done (or that we hope He will do) for us? Are we so well pleased with Jesus, and is He our beloved Savior in good times and in bad? It's something we would do well to consider.

As Jesus began His earthly ministry, He was baptized by John, the Holy Spirit descended like a dove upon Him, and the Father spoke to Him words of profound love and delight. How encouraging that must have been for Jesus, bracing Him for the long, difficult days ahead.

One final thought here: Do we often enough express our pleasure and delight to those close to us? Do they regularly hear words from us of affirmation and appreciation for who they are, irrespective of what they do or accomplish? Or are such words of endearment conditional, based on their good behavior or their success in some endeavor?

Someone I once knew repeated a well-worn cliché, to the point that I tired of hearing it. "You catch more flies with honey than with vinegar." But there is truth to that phrase, in the sense that positive words of delight and love encourage others more than we can even imagine. It is important that those we love hear such things from us regularly. Let's not assume that they know it. Tell them—every day. Even God the Father spoke from heaven to affirm God the Son. Let's not take it for granted. Our encouragement can have a profound influence for the positive.

Years ago, Dr. Tony Campolo related an interesting story. Miss Thompson taught Teddy Stallard in the fourth grade. He was a slow, unkempt student. He was a loner who was shunned by his classmates. The previous year his mother had died and what little motivation for school he may have once had was now gone.

Miss Thompson didn't particularly care for Teddy either, but at Christmastime he brought her a small present. Her desk was covered with beautiful, well-wrapped presents from the other children; but Teddy's came in a crumpled brown paper sack. When she opened it there was a gaudy rhinestone bracelet with half the stones missing and a bottle of cheap perfume.

The children began to snicker, but Miss Thompson saw the importance of the moment and quickly splashed on some perfume and put on the bracelet. She pretended that Teddy had given her some priceless relics.

At the end of the day Teddy worked up the courage to softly say, "Miss Thompson, you smell just like my mother, and her bracelet looks pretty on you, too. I'm glad you like my presents." After Teddy left, Miss Thompson got down on her knees and prayed for God's forgiveness. She prayed for God to use her to not only teach these children, but to love and to encourage them as well. She became a new teacher. She lovingly and patiently helped students like Teddy and by the end of the year he had caught up with most of the students.

Miss Thompson didn't hear from Teddy for a long time, then she received this note: "Dear Miss Thompson, I wanted you to be the first to know. I will be graduating second in my class. Love, Teddy Stallard." Four years later she got another note. "Dear Miss Thompson, They just told me I will be graduating first in my class. The university has not been easy, but I liked it. Love, Teddy Stallard." Four years later: "Dear Miss Thompson, As of today I am Theodore Stallard, M.D. How about that? I wanted you to be the first to know. I am getting married next month, the 27th to be exact. I want you to come and sit where my mother would sit if she were alive. You are the only family I have now; Dad died last year. Love, Teddy Stallard."[86]

Miss Thompson went to the wedding and sat where Teddy's mother would have sat because she let God use her as an instrument of encouragement. How many lives might we be able to influence in a positive way with our encouragement and affirmation? Only God knows!

QUESTIONS FOR CONTEMPLATION OR CONVERSATION

1. Does it surprise you that Jesus came to John to be baptized? Why or why not? Why do you think Jesus did so?

2. Have you ever deeply repented of your sin and fallen at the feet of Jesus for forgiveness? What led to that moment of divine encounter? What was the result?

3. What does the title "Son of God" when applied to Jesus mean to you? Is it part of the focus of your relationship with Him? Why or why not?

4. What words would you use to describe your love for your spouse, children and/or grandchildren? Can you even imagine the love of God for His Son?

5. Who in your life has been a person who has been a source of regular affirmation and encouragement for you, expressing their delight in who you are? How can you thank them?

6. To whom should you do a better job of expressing affirmation and delight? How can you begin to do so?

CHAPTER 11

The Beloved Son of God—2

"After six days Jesus took with Him Peter, James and John the brother of James, and led them up a high mountain by themselves. There He was transfigured before them. His face shone like the sun, and His clothes became as white as the light. Just then there appeared before them Moses and Elijah, talking with Jesus. Peter said to Jesus, 'Lord, it is good for us to be here. If you wish, I will put up three shelters—one for You, one for Moses and one for Elijah.' While he was still speaking, a bright cloud enveloped them, and a voice from the cloud said, 'This is My Son, whom I love; with Him I am well pleased. Listen to Him!'" (Matthew 17:1-5)

Now we move to the Mount of Transfiguration. This glorious event happened much later in Jesus' ministry, as He was preparing to head towards Jerusalem and the certainty of His crucifixion. Peter, James, and John were privileged to be invited up to a high mountain with Jesus, to witness an amazing sight and to hear the voice of God.

While they were on the mountain, Jesus was *"transfigured."* The Greek word was *metamorphōthē*—He was metamorphosed.[87] It means "to remodel," "to change into another form."[88] That was some kind of remodeling! I think of a family remodeling their home, which usually involves mostly an aesthetic change—new carpet, wall covering, perhaps new cabinets, maybe sometimes even an addition. But it is still the same basic house.

This was a total metamorphosis. His face shone like the sun. "It shone as the sun when He goes forth in His strength, so clear, so bright; for He is the Sun of righteousness, the Light of the world."[89] Moses' face shone brightly when he came down from the mountain and his meeting with God, so radiantly in fact that the people were afraid to come near.

> *"When Moses came down from Mount Sinai with the two tablets of the Testimony in his hands, he was not aware that his face was radiant because he had spoken with the Lord. When Aaron and all the Israelites saw Moses, his face was radiant, and they were afraid to come near him." (Exodus 34:29-30)*

I would assume Jesus' glorious radiance would have been even more amazing. His clothes also became white as the light.

When Saul (later to be known as Paul) was traveling to Damascus in his hunt to arrest and persecute Christians, suddenly a light from heaven shone around him. He fell to the ground in fear and wonder. It was Jesus in His radiant glory, and the light of it was so bright that Saul was blinded by it (Acts 9:1-9). Someday, after we are fully sanctified and have been given our eternal bodies, we may be physically able and allowed to see Christ in all His brilliant glory.

Jesus' appearance was changed right in front of the disciples. What an awesome sight it was that they were blessed to see! How overwhelmed, and stunned—even frightened?—they must have been. He had come to earth in the form of a human, putting aside His natural divine glory; now that heavenly glory was revealed before their very eyes.

And here's an aspect of this that is equally amazing. We, too, are to be likewise metamorphosed! We, too, are to be changed and remodeled into His likeness.

> *"And we, who with unveiled faces all reflect the Lord's glory, are being transformed into His likeness with ever-increasing glory, which comes from the Lord, who is the Spirit." (2 Corinthians 3:18)*

In the process theologians call "sanctification," we who have trusted in Jesus as Savior and are submitting to Him as Lord are being remade to become more and more like Him. The same Greek word used to describe Jesus' transfiguration in Matthew 17, was used by the Apostle Paul to express our own transformation into Christ-likeness.

We, of course, do not reveal divine glory as Jesus did, because we are not God like He is. So we will not shine with heavenly brightness and our clothes will not glow. And our transformation is not immediate, as was His. Ours is a lifelong process of maturation. We are to be growing in our faith and life to become more pure and godly, day by day.

The moment when we come to faith in Christ is not the end of our spiritual transformation, it is the beginning. Dr. Gaines S. Dobbins enjoyed a long tenure as professor of religious education at Southern Baptist Theological Seminary. Someone once asked him, "Is not conversion the end of evangelism?" Dr. Dobbins replied, "Yes. But which end?"[90] His point was that conversion is merely the beginning of the faith journey, and once we trust in Christ as Savior we have a long way to go to reach maturity.

The journey will likely involve stops and starts, many detours, hills and winding paths. It is not for most an easy passage. It will most likely involve unlearning things we have long assumed to be truth, but are not. There will be new attitudes and beliefs with which to get comfortable, countless insights to receive from Christ and likely many sins to overcome along the way. No matter our age or how long we have been at it, there is always still more to learn and assimilate.

The process will not end until the very day of our glorification, when, as Paul said it in 1 Corinthians 15, we will be raised in Christ imperishable, and the mortal will be replaced with the immortal (1 Corinthians 15:50-54). When the trumpet sounds we will be changed into our eternal fullness, but even in eternity I suspect we will continue to learn and grow.

The wonderful thought here is that, even as Christ was transfigured to reveal His heavenly glory, so we are being transformed and will one day become fully glorified in the Kingdom of God. What an overwhelming reality to anticipate. I cannot even imagine what it will be like to finally become what God created me to be, to put aside all the weight of sin to which I have grown so accustomed, and to be "remodeled" into the likeness of Christ.

But even that's not the end of the story. Moses and Elijah appeared to confer with Jesus. I wonder what was said—we aren't given that detail in Scripture. I imagine that they were there to support and encourage Him for the difficult task ahead. How amazing it will be in the glory of God's kingdom to speak with men like Moses and Elijah, Abraham and Isaac, David and Joshua—assuming we will have that ability—to hear their stories first hand, and to thank them for their amazing faithfulness to the purposes of God.

This was an awesome, overwhelming experience, to be sure. In fact, good old Peter, in his usual misguided enthusiasm, offered to build booths as memorials for Jesus, Moses, and Elijah so that all of them could remain there and enjoy the glory! I can relate to his enthusiasm, as perhaps can you. Over the years, we have participated in spiritual retreats, teaching seminars or sacred prayer gatherings, which left us on a "spiritual high" that we wished could have lasted forever. We would have liked to have stayed.

Peter wanted to stay on that mountain and bask in his own spiritual high as well. But he was interrupted before he could hire an architect or begin construction on his shrines by the crowning moment of the whole mountain experience—God the Father Himself spoke, audibly for all to hear. A bright cloud enveloped them.

Often in the Old Testament, a cloud was the visible token of God's presence. He came down upon Mount Sinai in a cloud (Exodus 19:9), and when He met with Moses, (Exodus 34:5 and Numbers 11:25, for instance) the LORD came in a cloud. When He was present in the Tent of Meeting it was in a cloud (e.g. Numbers 16:42-45); and when He took possession of the Temple it was in a cloud (1 Kings 8:10).

Here on the mount of Jesus' transfiguration, God revealed His divine power and presence in a cloud that "enveloped" them. It "overshadowed" them, surrounded and covered them. They were enfolded by the very visible, tangible presence of God.

Have you ever experienced God's very real presence in a cloud? Or maybe it was just in a quiet awareness that He was very near to you in a moment of profound worship; or in a significant insight from His Word; or in an awe-inspiring scene of His creative power and glory.

On some clear nights when I see the grandeur of a star-filled sky, I am touched by a sense of His presence and my own insignificance in the grand scheme of things. In fact, I have often said that the beginnings of my faith were in my appreciation for nature. I was awed by the beauty of the world around me, and realized that it all had to have a cause and a "Causer." It could not all have just happened by chance, as some are prone to believe; and from that simple realization came the awareness that we are not alone in this universe. There is a God, and we would do well to seek Him, worship Him and bow in submission to Him.

How amazing must it have been for the disciples of Jesus to stand in such proximity to the tangible cloud of the presence of God! I wonder what they thought in that moment. I wonder how they felt. The Scripture doesn't directly tell us, other than to relate Peter's bumbling attempt to memorialize the spot, which at least tells us that they were deeply moved and filled with wonder, wanting to do something to maintain the experience in some way.

But it wasn't only the cloud of God's presence that highlighted the scene—there was also His audible voice. God spoke, verbally, clearly, and perceptibly. They heard Him. For our purpose here in this volume, we want to notice particularly what God said. He spoke to and about His Son again, using much the same words as He did at Jesus' baptism—*"This is My Son, Whom I love; with Him I am well pleased."* In that first sentence it is word for word identical to that earlier expression.

But then God added a crucial phrase that the disciples (and we) would do well to hear: *"Listen to Him!"* The Greek word means "to listen," "to hear," and "to pay attention."[91] Jesus would often preface a teaching, or conclude it, by saying, *"He who has ears, let him hear."* (Matthew 11:15, 13:9, 15:10; Mark 4:9, 4:23; etc.) Another even more common phrase Jesus used to call people to pay attention to what He was about to say was *"I tell you the truth."* (NIV) The NASB has it as *"Truly I say to you,"* and the KJV translates it as *"Verily I say unto thee."* (Matthew 5:18, 5:26, 6:5; Luke 21:3; John 1:51; and many others) In these many instances, Jesus was essentially telling people to listen up, pay attention, and hear what He was about to say.

For many years we were involved in an after-school Bible Club in a local elementary school. After a day of schoolwork, the children came to us for another hour and a half of Bible lessons, crafts, and games. It was hard sometimes to get them to settle down and pay attention. I was always saying (loudly, to be heard over the din) "Listen up!" That, in essence, is what God said on the mount of transfiguration: "Listen to Him!" That, in essence, is what Jesus said so often to the crowds that surrounded Him: "I tell you the truth…verily I say unto thee…listen up!"

In Acts 3, Peter and John healed a lame beggar as they entered the Temple. All the people who saw this or heard about it were astonished and came running to them in the place called Solomon's Colonnade. When Peter saw this, he said to them:

> *"For Moses said, 'The Lord your God will raise up for you a Prophet like me from among your own people; <u>you must listen to everything He tells you</u>. Anyone who does not listen to Him will be completely cut off from among His people.'" (Acts 3:22-23, emphasis mine)*

Peter was saying that Jesus was the fulfillment of the prophecy of Moses. Jesus was the Prophet Whom God raised up from among His own people. Jesus is God with us.

How crucial it is for us to listen carefully to every word He had to say while He was on this earth. His words were (and are) truth. His words were (and are) divine. His words were (and are) eternal and infallible. There are those who dispute this. There are many who deny the inerrancy of the words of Jesus, and even like to debate whether or not the quotes recorded in Scripture really were the words of Christ. God said, simply, *"Listen to Him."* Pay attention. Hear Him.

Peter, in his sermon, took the words of Moses and applied them to Jesus, saying, "You must listen to *everything* He tells you. Anyone who does not listen to Him will be completely cut off from among His people." Evidently, Peter thought it critical that we listen and hear the teachings of Jesus.

The Apostle Paul agreed:

> *"How, then, can they call on the One they have not believed in? And how can they believe in the One of Whom they have not heard? And how can they hear without someone preaching to them? And how can they preach unless they are sent? As it is written, 'How beautiful are the feet of those who bring good news!'" (Romans 10:14-15)*

So we need to hear and listen to the Word of God in Christ in order to come to a saving faith to begin with. We must also hear and listen to the Word of God in Christ in order to grow and mature in that faith, to stay firmly in the truth and to stand against evil and wrong. God said it—and Matthew recorded it in His Gospel, as did Mark (Mark 9), as did Luke (Luke 9). Jesus said it. Peter said it. Paul said it. How much more often do we need to be told?

It should go without saying that to hear and listen is not enough. We must also *believe* and take it to heart. Paul talked above about that aspect of belief, using a word that means: "to believe to the extent of complete trust and reliance—to have confidence in, to have faith in, to trust."[92] I can listen to something and hear it well, without taking any of it to heart or believing it to be true or relevant to my life. It is clear that here we are talking about hearing and believing. God called us to listen, hear and believe His Son.

I guess the question for us is: Are we hearing the Word of God? Are we reading it and studying it? Are we hearing it preached on any regular basis? Are we paying attention and listening, truly? Or are we listening to what we read online, or in the mainline media, or from friends and peers? And are we trusting and believing what His Word tells us?

John Quincy Adams said:

> *"I have for many years made it a practice to read through the Bible once a year. My custom is to read four or five chapters every morning immediately after rising from my bed. It employs about an hour of my time, and seems to me the most suitable manner of beginning the day. In what light soever we regard the Bible, whether with reference to revelation, to history, or to morality, it is an invaluable and inexhaustible mine of knowledge and virtue."*[93]

He gave the study of Scripture an hour a day of his time, even as a busy patriot, diplomat and President of the United States and found it to be "invaluable." What about us? How much time do we give most days to hearing, listening and paying attention to God's Word? It's an important consideration.

The Beloved Son of God—Part 2

> *"In the past God spoke to our forefathers through the prophets at many times and in various ways, but in these last days He has spoken to us by His Son, Whom He appointed heir of all things, and through Whom He made the universe. The Son is the radiance of God's glory and the exact representation of His being, sustaining all things by His powerful Word." (Hebrews 1:1-3)*

There is one further aspect of this that we MUST consider. The Greek word in the text for this chapter, from Matthew 17:5—*akouete*—means more than just to listen or even to pay attention. It means: "to listen or pay attention to a person, with resulting conformity to what is advised or commanded—to pay attention to *and* obey."[94] God was saying in essence, "This is My Son, whom I love; with Him I am well pleased. Listen to Him and obey Him!" Jesus Himself reiterated this very point.

> *"Why do you call me, 'Lord, Lord,' and do not do what I say?"* (Luke 6:46)

The point here is *obedience*. It is not enough just to listen, pay attention and hear Jesus' Word. It's not enough to blithely call Him "Lord." We must also do what He commands us to do. Unquestioning obedience is what He calls for from us.

It is often said that, next to the one who does not pay his bill, the doctor's most annoying patient is the one who refuses to follow orders. Recently it was estimated that between 16 to *90* percent of all patients leave half-empty pill bottles, cheat on diets, continue to smoke or never return for checkups despite careful prescriptions and cautious advice.[95] How many of us, who claim the name of Christ, faithfully strive to do all that He says to us?

In Genesis 32 we read a mysterious story about Jacob, as he was returning to Canaan after many years in exile for fear of his brother Esau's revenge. Along the way, he wrestled with "a man," who in Hosea is called an angel (Hosea 12:4), but there in Genesis 32 is referred to as God Himself (Genesis 32:28 and 30). Whoever it was (I think it was God!), He eventually touched the socket of Jacob's hip so that it was dislocated. It is assumed that

Jacob walked with a limp for the rest of his life, a constant reminder of this close encounter with the Lord.

Have you ever wondered why God specifically touched Jacob on the hip? A physician once explained. The sinew of the thigh is the strongest in the human body. God had to break Jacob down at the strongest part of his independent self-reliance in order to have His way with Jacob.[96]

The same could most likely be said of us. God needs to break through our perceived self-sufficiency in order to force us to accept His divine sovereignty over our lives. Only when we fully acknowledge Jesus as our Savior and truly bow before Him as our Lord can we begin to learn the obedience God called for on the Mount of Transfiguration. Only then will we call Him "Lord, Lord," and at least try to do what He says.

QUESTIONS FOR CONTEMPLATION OR CONVERSATION

1. Imagine in your mind how Jesus might have looked after His transfiguration? What words would you use to describe Him? How might this be like His appearance in heaven?

2. How might you have reacted if you had been on the Mount of Transfiguration? Can you relate to Peter's response?

3. When have you experienced moments of extreme spiritual highs? What were the occasions and how did you respond to them?

4. Who, other than Jesus, would you especially look forward to speaking with in eternity? Why?

5. In what ways do you truly "listen" to Jesus? What works best for you to hear from Him and understand His voice?

6. Rate your level of obedience to Jesus and His Word from one to ten, ten being perfectly, one being very little. Assuming that few of us would presume to say ten, what could you do to increase your level of submission to Him?

CHAPTER 12

Superior to All Others

"For to which of the angels did God ever say, 'You are My Son; today I have become Your Father?' Or again, 'I will be His Father, and He will be My Son?' And again, when God brings His firstborn into the world, He says, 'Let all God's angels worship Him.' In speaking of the angels He says, 'He makes His angels winds, His servants flames of fire.'

But about the Son He says, 'Your throne, O God, will last for ever and ever, and righteousness will be the scepter of Your kingdom. You have loved righteousness and hated wickedness; therefore God, Your God, has set You above Your companions by anointing You with the oil of joy.'

He also says, 'In the beginning, O Lord, You laid the foundations of the earth, and the heavens are the work of Your hands. They will perish, but You remain; they will all wear out like a garment. You will roll them up like a robe; like a garment they will be changed. But You remain the same, and Your years will never end.'

To which of the angels did God ever say, 'Sit at My right hand until I make Your enemies a footstool for Your feet?'" (Hebrews 1:5-13)

To better understand the passage above, it would be best to read Hebrews 1 beginning at verse 1. There we would see that the basic point being made at the beginning of this anonymous epistle (no one knows for certain who wrote it—possibilities abound) is that Jesus is infinitely superior to anyone else, even the angels.

The word *better* is used thirteen times in this book as the writer shows the superiority of Jesus Christ and His salvation over the Hebrew system of religion. The epistle says: Christ is *"much superior to the angels"* (Hebrews 1:4); He introduced *"a better hope"* (Hebrews 7:19); because He is the Mediator of a superior covenant, which was founded on better promises (Hebrews 8:6).[97]

"In ages past God spoke to His people through the patriarchs and prophets, at many times and in various ways." (Hebrews 1:1) But then He spoke through the incarnation, life, death and resurrection of Jesus, the Son. Jesus shows us the Father's character and being infinitely more clearly than anyone or anything else, past or present. So He is much superior to all others, even the angels. So the epistle of Hebrews began.

There followed a series of several quotations from the Old Testament, each used to buttress the thesis that Christ is far superior to any other. All are affirmations endorsing the Lord Jesus and are represented as things that the Father Himself said about the Son; which means this section of Holy Scripture fits quite well into our theme for this volume. So, in Hebrews 1, what did God say—about Jesus? We will take them one at a time.

He is the Son of God.

> *"For to which of the angels did God ever say,*
> *'You are My Son; today I have become Your Father?'*
> *Or again, 'I will be His Father, and He will be My Son?'"*
> *(Hebrews 1:5)*

This is quoting Psalm 2:

> *"I will proclaim the decree of the* Lord*:*
> *He said to Me, 'You are my Son;*
> *today I have become Your Father.'" (Psalm 2:7)*

We discussed this in Chapter 10. Jesus is the Beloved Son of God from before the beginning of time, in a sense no one else ever has been or will be. Angels are called "the sons of God" in Job 1:6 (The NIV uses the word "angels," but the Hebrew is "sons of God."). The faithful children of Seth are called "sons of God," in Genesis 6:2 and 4. Hosea even used the phrase to refer to all who stand in relation to God by His grace.[98] And the New Testament uses this phrase to speak of all who have come to God through faith in Christ, as in 2 Corinthians:

> *"I will be a Father to you, and you will be My sons and daughters, says the Lord Almighty." (2 Corinthians 6:18)*

Those references are in the plural sense, talking about a group of people in special relationship with God. This reference in Hebrews is singular, with a capital "S." Jesus is the infinite, divine, second person of the Holy Trinity "Son of God," which is reaffirmed here yet again by God Himself.

We need to understand and acknowledge that Jesus is part of the divine, eternal, holy, triune God, and reverence Him as such. He is not our "buddy," "pal," "copilot" or "the Big Guy in the sky." He is God.

He is worshiped by the angels.

> *"And again, when God brings His firstborn into the world, He [God] says, 'Let all God's angels worship Him.'" (Hebrews 1:6)*

Scholars tell us that the writer quoted from the Greek version of the Hebrew Old Testament, known as the *Septuagint*. (The word *Septuagint* is a Greek word that means "seventy.") Tradition claims that seventy men translated the Hebrew Old Testament into the Greek. The abbreviation for *Septuagint* is LXX. So this is a quote of Deuteronomy 32:43 in the LXX: "Heavens, rejoice with Him, let the sons of God pay Him homage!"[99]

Here, as elsewhere, the term *"firstborn"* is not a reference to birth order, as in the first child born of many, or the first progeny of a husband and wife. Often this is simply a term of honor and place, denoting a rank of highest privilege and status.

As the firstborn Son of God, there is no one higher than Jesus Christ, and God the Father commands the angels to worship Him. As one commentator says it, "God commanded them to do so, which proves that Jesus Christ is God; for none of God's angels would worship a mere creature."[100]

If the angels are commanded to worship Him, how much more should we? As they worship Him in heaven, we are to worship Him on earth, giving Him the praise He so richly deserves. In fact, we can never give Him all the glory He should have, but we are to do our best to lift Jesus in prayer and song. As the old Charles Wesley hymn says it:

> *"O for a thousand tongues to sing*
> *My great Redeemer's praise,*
> *The glories of my God and King*
> *The triumphs of His grace."*

He is God's anointed, eternal King.

"But about the Son He [God] says, 'Your throne, O God, will last for ever and ever, and righteousness will be the scepter of Your kingdom. You have loved righteousness and hated wickedness; therefore God, Your God, has set You above Your companions by anointing You with the oil of joy." (Hebrews 1:8-9)

This, a quote from Psalm 45:6-7, tells us that Jesus' throne will be eternal—*"for ever and ever."* When Jesus ascended to heaven He was anointed by God with the *"oil of joy."* Imagine the celebration and joy there must have been on that day when the Son returned home to the Father, after all the pain, sorrow, agony, humiliation, and separation of His human, earthly life. Like the party the father threw in Jesus' parable about the Prodigal Son (Luke 15:11-31), except that (unlike the young man in Jesus' parable) Christ was certainly not irresponsible or reckless in any way. He had left His home in heaven to do the Father's will for our salvation. But now He was home, having faithfully completed the task to which He had been called.

With great joy and gladness Jesus was enthroned in heaven, given once again His rightful place in glory, where the angels worship and serve Him and the saints sing His praise. During Jesus' trial before the Sanhedrin, the high priest asked Him, *"Are You the Christ, the Son of the Blessed One?"* And Jesus answered: *"I am...And you will see the Son of Man sitting at the right hand of the Mighty One and coming on the clouds of heaven."* (Mark 14:61-62)

Jesus knew, even as He faced torture, crucifixion and death, that He was headed home, and an eternal throne awaited Him there. The celebration continues even as we speak, for the King reigns, now and forever!

When Jesus returns to earth to judge and make war against the enemies of God, Revelation 19 gives a striking portrait of Him. His eyes will be like blazing fire, on His head will be many crowns, He will be dressed in a robe dipped in blood and He will be followed by the great armies of heaven.

"On His robe and on His thigh He has this name written: KING OF KINGS AND LORD OF LORDS.*" (Revelation 19:16)*

He is Creator of all.

"He [God] also says, 'In the beginning, O Lord, You laid the foundations of the earth, and the heavens are the work of Your hands. They will perish, but You remain; they will all wear out like a garment. You will roll them up like a robe; like a garment they will be changed. But You remain the same, and Your years will never end." (Hebrews 1:10-12)

This quotation comes from Psalm 102:25-27. It states clearly that Jesus Christ is the Creator, repeating the truth of John 1:

"In the beginning was the Word, and the Word was with God, and the Word was God. He was with God in the beginning. Through Him all things were made; without Him nothing was made that has been made." (John 1:1-3)

This refutes the current secular humanist view that the universe sprang into being by random chance and that there was no God to call it into being.

Here God Himself speaks of the Son as the One Who laid the foundations of the earth and the One Who brought forth the heavens themselves. Any secular theory of creation (the "Big Bang," Darwinian evolution, or any other) that does not acknowledge God as the origin of the universe is incomplete and false.

> *"Yet for us there is but one God, the Father, from Whom all things came and for Whom we live; and there is but one Lord, Jesus Christ, through Whom all things came and through Whom we live." (1 Corinthians 8:6)*

> *"For from Him [Jesus] and through Him and to Him are all things. To Him be the glory forever! Amen." (Romans 11:36)*

> *"For by Him [Jesus] all things were created: things in heaven and on earth, visible and invisible, whether thrones or powers or rulers or authorities; all things were created by Him and for Him." (Colossians 1:16)*

There is a Creator, and Jesus is the agent of that creation. God makes that clear here and elsewhere in His eternal Word.

A child (or a child in Christ) may think in basic terms of God the Father as Creator, God the Son as Savior and God the Holy Spirit as Helper. But that is too simplistic a way to describe the unity within the Holy Trinity. All Three were present and involved in Creation, and one day He will do away with the old creation and bring in a new creation. "Creation is like an old garment, which will one day be discarded in favor of a new one."[101] As believers we anticipate with joyous expectation that glorious day when all things will be made right and new!

He rules at the right hand of the Father.

> *"To which of the angels did God ever say, 'Sit at My right hand until I make Your enemies a footstool for Your feet?' Are not all angels ministering spirits sent to serve those who will inherit salvation?" (Hebrews 1:13-14)*

Here we see a quote of Psalm 110:1. We are told by God that Jesus has been invited to sit at the right hand of God in the throne room of heaven until the Father makes all Jesus' enemies His footstool. What does that mean? In ancient days, when a victorious king conquered his enemy in battle, he would put his foot on the neck of the vanquished foe as a sign of his dominance and their humiliation. They would be, in essence, a footstool for the triumphant warrior.

All the enemies of Christ will become His conquered footstools, just like that. Those who have worshiped and served false gods and false religions; those who have worked so hard to deny Him, defeat His purposes, destroy His Church and the faith itself; those who have so zealously and diligently attempted to marginalize and minimize the influence of His Gospel in the culture; those who mocked and persecuted Jesus and His people—all will one day bow before Him.

We will all one day lie prostrate before Him. Some will do so in worship and awe, bowing at His feet in reverent worship. Others will fall to their faces in fear and regret, terrified at the coming judgment which will be their due. As Matthew Henry said it in his commentary:

> "All the enemies of Christ shall be made His footstool, either by humble submission and entire subjection to His will casting themselves down at His feet, or by utter destruction; He shall trample upon those who continue obstinate, and shall trample over them."[102]

We have the choice: to bow at His feet in reverence and gratitude for His saving grace, or to tremble in the face of His just fury. As the epistle to the Hebrews so effectively argues, Jesus is infinitely superior to the angels or to anyone else. Why would we ever want to worship or serve an inferior false god in this life, and face His judgment in the next?

QUESTIONS FOR CONTEMPLATION OR CONVERSATION

1. In what ways is Jesus better to you than anyone or anything on this earth?

2. What words would you use to describe who Jesus is to you? Are they reverent or perhaps too casual?

3. "If the angels are commanded to worship Him, how much more should we?" How do you worship and praise Him? Is it as much as He deserves?

4. Jesus is "KING OF KINGS AND LORD OF LORDS." (Revelation 19:16) What do you do in your daily life to bow before Him as your King? What more could you do?

5. Do you think of Christ as Creator? Do you normally understand Him as being active in the creation event? Why or why not?

6. Do you anticipate with joy one day bowing at Jesus' feet in reverent awe and worship; or do you see that as a day of fear and regret, terrified at the coming judgment? Why? What can you do about that?

CONCLUSION

The Testimony of the Father

"I have testimony weightier than that of John. For the very work that the Father has given Me to finish, and which I am doing, testifies that the Father has sent Me. And the Father who sent Me has Himself testified concerning Me. You have never heard His voice nor seen His form, nor does His word dwell in you, for you do not believe the one He sent. You diligently study the Scriptures because you think that by them you possess eternal life. These are the Scriptures that testify about Me, yet you refuse to come to Me to have life." (John 5:36-40)

The Jewish leaders were trying to find cause and opportunity to kill Jesus, not only because He was breaking their Sabbath rules and regulations, but because He was calling God His Father and making Himself equal with God (John 5:18). To them that was blasphemous and punishable by death.

Jesus did not argue with their basic accusation. In fact He *agreed* with them. He openly admitted that He was claiming to be equal with God in the works that He did on earth, in His role as judge over humankind, and in His ability to raise people to new and eternal life (John 5:19-30). Jesus even acknowledged that according to Jewish law, His own word was not enough to establish that fact. *"If I testify about Myself, My testimony is not valid."* (John 5:31) It was common knowledge among the Jews that two or three witnesses were required.

"One witness is not enough to convict a man accused of any crime or offense he may have committed. A matter must be established by the testimony of two or three witnesses." (Deuteronomy 19:15)

So, as recorded in John 5, Jesus spoke of three clear and crucial witnesses to His deity. The first was John the Baptist. John faithfully prepared the way for the coming of the Messiah, and then loudly declared Christ as the One.

"The next day John saw Jesus coming toward him and said, 'Look, the Lamb of God, who takes away the sin of the world!'" (John 1:29)

"I have seen and I testify that this is the Son of God." (John 1:34)

Of course, not everyone believed John to be the herald of the Savior, so Jesus referred to a second witness: the works that He did. The countless miraculous healings, feeding the great multitudes with just a few loaves and fishes (more than once), casting out so many demons, walking on water, stilling the storm—too many examples of divine power to even begin to enumerate. The Apostle John even quoted them as proofs of Jesus' deity.

"Jesus did many other miraculous signs in the presence of His disciples, which are not recorded in this book. But these are written that you may believe that Jesus is the Christ, the Son of God, and that by believing you may have life in His name." (John 20:30-31)

But even that was not enough to convince many. Many still doubted, questioned and refused to believe Him. So Jesus held up one more witness, the third: God Himself. *"And the Father who sent Me has Himself testified concerning Me."* (John 5:37) That's what we have been briefly studying in this overview—God's own testimony about His Son.

The Holy Bible is God's Word in written form. The Hebrew word is *dābār*; the Greek is *logos*.[103] The concept of the Word of God covers much more than mere spoken sounds; it is God's truth, reason and creative, ordering power being revealed from His person. That powerful Word was given to us through the patriarchs and prophets, through the Bible, and through creation itself.

But the highest and best form of the revelation of the Word—was Jesus. Jesus was God's Word in human form. Earlier we quoted from Hebrews 1, which reminds us:

"In the past God spoke to our forefathers through the prophets at many times and in various ways, but in these last days He has spoken to us by His Son, whom He appointed heir of all things, and through whom He made the universe. The Son is the radiance of God's glory and the exact representation of His being, sustaining all things by His powerful word." (Hebrews 1:1-3)

He was (and is) the radiance of the Father's glory. He was (and is) the clearest disclosure of God's being and truth. We also quoted from Revelation 19, which tells us about Christ returning to earth in power and glory at the end of time. There it says:

"He is dressed in a robe dipped in blood, and His name is the Word of God." (Revelation 19:13)

And in the written Word of God we hear His witness that Jesus is His Son and the Savior of humankind. What we have seen in the previous pages is God's own testimony concerning His Son. This is Who Jesus is according to the Father, not the imagination of men's mind, not the ramblings of our post-modern secular culture. Jesus Himself pointed to the Word of His Father to verify His own character and deity. We have turned to that Word to learn the truth of Who Jesus is.

One thing remains: to hear, believe and respond to Him in faith and trust. If you have never truly invited Him to become your own personal Savior and Lord, the following is a simple invitation I have used over the years to encourage people to make a decision for their own eternal destiny:

ALL ARE SINNERS. No one is perfect, except for Jesus, the Son. Everyone else in human history, including me and you, continuously and daily (perhaps hourly) commit thoughts and acts of disobedience against the holy character and Word of God. We must first acknowledge and admit our sinfulness, and recognize that we deserve God's just wrath.

> Romans 3:23—"For all have sinned and fall short of the glory of God."
>
> Romans 6:23—"For the wages of sin is death..."

BELIEVE THAT JESUS DIED FOR YOUR SINS. When Jesus went to the cross, He paid the penalty for our sin and guilt that we ourselves justly deserve. Secondly, we need to accept that Jesus did for us what we could never do for ourselves—fulfill the just judgment of the holy and righteous God required of us because of our guilt.

> Romans 6:23—"...but the gift of God is eternal life in Christ Jesus our Lord."
>
> Romans 5:8—"But God demonstrates His love for us in this: while we were still sinners, Christ died for us."
>
> 1 John 5:11—"And this is the testimony: God has given us eternal life, and this life is in His Son."

CONFESS YOUR SINS, and by faith accept God's free gift of salvation. Thirdly, we must accept what Jesus did on our behalf as our personal Savior, praying to acknowledge Him as our Savior and Lord.

> Romans 10:9—"That if you confess with your mouth, 'Jesus is Lord,' and believe in your heart that God raised Him from the dead, you will be saved."
>
> Romans 10:13—"For everyone who calls on the name of the Lord will be saved."

WHAT TO PRAY

Dear Lord Jesus,

I know that I am a sinner and need Your forgiveness. I believe that You died for my sins. I want to turn from my sins. I now invite You to come into my heart and life. I want to trust You and follow You as Lord and Savior. Amen.

If you have sincerely prayed a prayer like that, and bowed before Jesus as Savior and Lord, praise be to God! Please find a good, Bible-based church to attend so you might grow in that faith and life, and find a Christian friend to walk with you in that journey. It is just the beginning of an eternal life of discovery and peace.

Endnotes

INTRODUCTION

1. D.R.W. Wood, I.H. Marshall, A.R. Millard, J.I. Packer, and D.J. Wiseman (Eds.), *New Bible Dictionary, Third Edition* (Downers Grove, IL: InterVarsity Press, 1996), 1209.

CHAPTER 1

2. D. Story, *Defending Your Faith* (Grand Rapids, MI: Kregel Publications, 1997), 203-204.
3. R.L. Thomas, *New American Standard Hebrew-Aramaic and Greek Dictionaries: Updated Edition* (Anaheim, CA: Foundation Publications, Inc., 1998), 5175.
4. R.C. Sproul, *The Holiness of God* (Wheaton, IL: Tyndale House Publishers, 1985), 151.
5. J.M. Freeman and H.J. Chadwick, *Manners and Customs of the Bible, Revised Edition* (North Brunswick, NJ: Bridge-Logos Publishers, 1984), 2.
6. F.L. Cross and E.A. Livingstone, *The Oxford Dictionary of the Christian Church, Third Edition Revised* (New York, NY: Oxford University Press, 2005), 830.
7. C.C. Ryrie, *A Survey of Bible Doctrine* (Chicago: Moody Press, 1995).
8. D. Strain, "God Is Infinite," *Tabletalk Magazine,* March 2020, volume 44, number 3, 57.
9. P.L. Tan, *Encyclopedia of 7700 Illustrations: Signs of the Times* (Garland TX: Bible Communications, Inc., 1996), 649.

CHAPTER 2

10. W.W. Wiersbe, *Wiersbe's Expository Outlines on the Old Testament* (Wheaton, IL: Victor Books, 1993), Genesis 49.
11. J.M. Freeman and H.J. Chadwick, *Manners and Customs of the Bible, Revised Edition* (North Brunswick, NJ: Bridge-Logos Publishers, 1998), 90-91.
12. F. Brown, S.R. Driver, and C.A. Briggs, *Enhanced Brown-Driver-Briggs Hebrew and English Lexicon* (Oxford: Clarendon Press, 1977), 1010.

13. J. Swanson, and O. Nave, *New Nave's Topical Bible* (Oak Harbor, WA: Logos Research Systems, 1994).
14. J.M. Freeman and H.J. Chadwick, *Manners and Customs of the Bible, Revised Edition* (North Brunswick, NJ: Bridge-Logos Publishers, 1998), 90-91.
15. Quoted in P.L. Tan, *Encyclopedia of 7700 Illustrations: Signs of the Times* (Garland, TX: Bible Communications, Inc., 1996), 508-509.
16. R.L. Thomas, *New American Standard Hebrew-Aramaic and Greek Dictionaries: Updated Edition* (Anaheim, CA: Foundation Publications, Inc., 1998).
17. P.L. Tan, *Encyclopedia of 7700 Illustrations: Signs of the Times* (Garland, TX: Bible Communications, Inc., 1996), 237.

CHAPTER 3

18. R.C. Sproul, ed., *New Geneva Study Bible, New King James Version* (Nashville, TN: Thomas Nelson, 1995), 1020.
19. F. Brown, S.R. Driver and C.A. Briggs, *Enhanced Brown-Driver-Briggs Hebrew and English Lexicon* (Oxford: Clarendon Press, 1977), 310.
20. F. Brown, S.R. Driver, and C.A. Briggs, *Enhanced Brown-Driver-Briggs Hebrew and English Lexicon* (Oxford: Clarendon Press, 1977), 315.
21. R. Jamieson, A.R. Fausset, and D. Brown, *Commentary Critical and Explanatory on the Whole Bible, Volume 2* (Oak Harbor, WA: Logos Research Systems, Inc., 1997), 376.
22. Ibid., 443.
23. J.F. Walvoord and R.B. Zuck, eds., *The Bible Knowledge Commentary: An Exposition of the Scriptures, Volume 1* (Wheaton, IL: Victor Books, 1983), 1056.
24. P.L. Tan, *Encyclopedia of 7700 Illustrations: Signs of the Times* (Garland, TX: Bible Communications, Inc., 1966), 270.

CHAPTER 4

25. J.F. Walvoord and R.B. Zuck, eds., *The Bible Knowledge Commentary: An Exposition of the Scriptures, Volume 1* (Wheaton, IL: Victor Books, 1983), 1077-1078.
26. R.L. Thomas, *New American Standard Hebrew-Aramaic and Greek Dictionaries: Updated Edition* (Anaheim, CA: Foundation Publications, Inc., 1998).
27. Ibid.

28. P.L. Tan, *Encyclopedia of 7700 Illustrations: Signs of the Times* (Garland, TX: Bible Communications, Inc., 1996), 673.

29. J. Swanson, *Dictionary of Biblical Languages with Semantic Domains: Hebrew (Old Testament), Electronic Edition* (Oak Harbor, WA: Logos Research Systems, Inc., 1997).

30. R. Jamieson, A.R. Fausset, and D. Brown, *Commentary Critical and Explanatory on the Whole Bible, Volume 1* (Oak Harbor, WA: Logos Research Systems, Inc., 1997), 461.

31. Merriam Webster, *Merriam-Webster's Collegiate Thesaurus, Electronic Edition* (Springfield, MA: Merriam-Webster, 1996).

32. P.L. Tan, *Encyclopedia of 7700 Illustrations: Signs of the Times* (Garland, TX: Bible Communications, Inc., 1996), 1513.

33. J.F. Walvoord and R.B. Zuck, eds., *The Bible Knowledge Commentary: An Exposition of the Scriptures, Volume 1* (Wheaton, IL: Victor Books, 1983), 1077-1078.

34. P.L. Tan, *Encyclopedia of 7700 Illustrations: Signs of the Times* (Garland, TX: Bible Communications, Inc., 1996), 993.

CHAPTER 5

35. J.E. Smith, *The Books of History* (Joplin, MO: College Press, 1995), 23.

36. R. Jamieson, A.R. Fausset, and D. Brown, *Commentary Critical and Explanatory on the Whole Bible, Volume 1* (Oak Harbor, WA: Logos Research Systems, Inc., 1997), 477.

37. P.L. Tan, *Encyclopedia of 7700 Illustrations: Signs of the Times* (Garland, TX: Bible Communications, Inc., 1996), 1232.

38. https://www.preachingtoday.com/illustrations/2012/june.

39. http://www.prayerfoundation.org/world.

40. J.M. Freeman and H.J. Chadwick, *Manners and Customs of the Bible, Revised Edition* (North Brunswick, NJ: Bridge-Logos Publishers, 1998), 361.

41. M. Henry, *Matthew Henry's Commentary on the Whole Bible: Complete and Unabridged in One Volume* (Peabody: Hendrickson, 1994), 1155-1156.

42. P.L. Tan, *Encyclopedia of 7700 Illustrations: Signs of the Times* (Garland, TX: Bible Communications, Inc., 1996), 702.

CHAPTER 6

43 R. Jamieson, A.R. Fausset, and D. Brown, *Commentary Critical and Explanatory on the Whole Bible, Volume 1* (Oak Harbor, WA: Logos Research Systems, Inc., 1997), 477.

44 R.L. Thomas, *New American Standard Hebrew-Aramaic and Greek Dictionaries: Updated Edition* (Anaheim, CA: Foundation Publications, Inc., 1998), 7121.

45 J.P. Louw and E.A. Nida, *Greek-English Lexicon of the New Testament: Based on Semantic Domains, Electronic Edition of the 2nd Edition, Volume 1* (New York: United Bible Societies, 1996), 482.

46 F. Brown, S.R. Driver, and C.A. Briggs, *Enhanced Brown-Driver-Briggs Hebrew and English Lexicon* (Oxford: Clarendon Press, 1977), 665.

47 W.W. Wiersbe, *The Bible Exposition Commentary, Volume 1* (Wheaton, IL: Victor Books, 1996), 103.

48 J.P. Louw and E.A. Nida, *Greek-English Lexicon of the New Testament: Based on Semantic Domains, Electronic Edition of the 2nd Edition, Volume 1* (New York: United Bible Societies, 1996), 447.

49 P.L. Tan, *Encyclopedia of 7700 Illustrations: Signs of the Times* (Garland, TX: Bible Communications, Inc., 1996), 520.

50 H.H. Hobbs, *My Favorite Illustrations* (Nashville, TN: Broadman Press, 1990), 237.

51 Ibid., 238.

52 W. Barclay, *The Gospel of Matthew, Volume 1; The Daily Bible Study Series* (Philadelphia, PA: The Westminster Press, 1975), 308.

53 R. Jamieson, A.R. Fausset, and D. Brown, *Commentary Critical and Explanatory on the Whole Bible, Volume 1* (Oak Harbor, WA: Logos Research Systems, Inc., 1997), 435.

CHAPTER 7

54 W.W. Wiersbe, *Be Decisive* (Wheaton, IL: Victor Books, 1996), 104-105.

55 W. Barclay, *The Gospel of Matthew, Volume 1; The Daily Bible Study Series* (Philadelphia, PA: The Westminster Press, 1975), 282.

56 J.D. Barry, D. Bomar, D.R. Brown, R. Klippenstein, D. Mangum, C. Sinclair Wolcott, W. Widder, eds., *The Lexham Bible Dictionary* (Bellingham, WA: Lexham Press, 2016).

57 R. Jamieson, A.R. Fausset, and D. Brown, *Commentary Critical and Explanatory on the Whole Bible, Volume 1* (Oak Harbor, WA: Logos Research Systems, Inc., 1997), 529.

58 J.D. Barry, D. Bomar, D.R. Brown, R. Klippenstein, D. Mangum, C. Sinclair Wolcott, W. Widder, eds., *The Lexham Bible Dictionary* (Bellingham, WA: Lexham Press, 2016).

59 D.S. Dockery, ed., *Holman Bible Handbook* (Nashville, TN: Holman Bible Publishers, 1992), 823.

60 J.P. Louw and E.A. Nida, *Greek-English Lexicon of the New Testament: Based on Semantic Domains, Electronic Edition of the 2nd Edition, Volume 1* (New York: United Bible Societies, 1996), 743.

61 W.W. Wiersbe, *The Bible Exposition Commentary, Volume 1* (Wheaton, IL: Victor Books, 1996), 572.

62 P.L. Tan, *Encyclopedia of 7700 Illustrations: Signs of the Times* (Garland, TX: Bible Communications, Inc., 1996), 1188.

CHAPTER 8

63 W.W. Wiersbe, *Wiersbe's Expository Outlines on the Old Testament* (Wheaton, IL: Victor Books, 1993), Daniel 7-8.

64 A.C. Myers in the *Eerdmans Bible Dictionary* (Grand Rapids, MI: Eerdmans, 1987), 962.

65 F.L. Cross and E.A., editors, *The Oxford Dictionary of the Christian Church*, 3rd edition revised (New York: Oxford University Press, 2005), 1529.

66 P.J. Achtemeier in *Harper's Bible Dictionary, 1st Edition* (San Francisco: Harper & Row, 1985), 981.

67 W.W. Wiersbe, *The Bible Exposition Commentary, Volume 2* (Wheaton, IL: Victor Books, 1996), 284.

68 H.H. Hobbs, *My Favorite Illustrations* (Nashville, TN: Broadman Press, 1990), 229.

69 P.L. Tan, *Encyclopedia of 7700 Illustrations: Signs of the Times* (Garland, TX: Bible Communications, Inc., 1996), 279.

70 C. Thomas, *America's Expiration Date: The Fall of Empires and Superpowers, and the Future of the United States* (Grand Rapids, MI: Zondervan, 2020).

71 P.L. Tan, *Encyclopedia of 7700 Illustrations: Signs of the Times* (Garland, TX: Bible Communications, Inc., 1996), 312–313.

CHAPTER 9

72 R. Jamieson, A.R. Fausset, and D. Brown, *Commentary Critical and Explanatory on the Whole Bible, Volume 1* (Oak Harbor, WA: Logos Research Systems, Inc., 1997), 692-693.

73 W.W. Wiersbe, *Wiersbe's Expository Outlines on the Old Testament* (Wheaton, IL: Victor Books, 1993), Micah 1-5.

74 M. Henry, *Matthew Henry's Commentary on the Whole Bible: Complete and Unabridged in One Volume* (Peabody: Hendrickson, 1994), 1539-1540.

75 P.L. Tan, *Encyclopedia of 7700 Illustrations: Signs of the Times* (Garland, TX: Bible Communications, Inc., 1996), 987.

76 H.H. Hobbs, *My Favorite Illustrations* (Nashville, TN: Broadman Press, 1990), 113.

77 Ibid., 171.

78 W.W. Wiersbe, *Wiersbe's Expository Outlines on the Old Testament* (Wheaton, IL: Victor Books, 1993), Micah 1-5.

CHAPTER 10

79 W.W. Wiersbe, *The Bible Exposition Commentary, Volume 1* (Wheaton, IL: Victor Books, 1996), 16.

80 M. Henry, *Matthew Henry's Commentary on the Whole Bible: Complete and Unabridged in One Volume* (Peabody: Hendrickson, 1994), 1621.

81 A.C. Myers, *The Eerdmans Bible Dictionary* (Grand Rapids, MI: Eerdmans, 1987), 961.

82 J.P. Louw and E.A. Nida, *Greek-English Lexicon of the New Testament: Based on Semantic Domains, Electronic Edition of the 2nd Edition, Volume 1* (New York: United Bible Societies, 1996), 590.

83 G. Kittel, G. W. Bromiley, and G. Friedrich, eds., *Theological Dictionary of the New Testament, Electronic Edition, Volume 4* (Grand Rapids, MI: Eerdmans), 738.

84 J.P. Louw and E.A. Nida, *Greek-English Lexicon of the New Testament: Based on Semantic Domains, Electronic Edition of the 2nd Edition, Volume 1* (New York: United Bible Societies, 1996), 590.

85 Ibid., 298.

86   T. Campolo, *Who Switched the Pricetags?* (Nashville, TN: Thomas Nelson,1986), 69-72.

CHAPTER 11

87   M. Henry, *Matthew Henry's Commentary on the Whole Bible: Complete and Unabridged in One Volume* (Peabody: Hendrickson, 1994), 1699.

88   G. Kittel, G.W. Bromiley, and G. Friedrich, eds., *Theological Dictionary of the New Testament, Electronic Edition, Volume 4* (Grand Rapids, MI: Eerdmans, 1967), 755.

89   M. Henry, *Matthew Henry's Commentary on the Whole Bible: Complete and Unabridged in One Volume* (Peabody: Hendrickson, 1994), 1700.

90   H.H. Hobbs, *My Favorite Illustrations* (Nashville, TN: Broadman Press, 1990), 34.

91   J.P. Louw and E.A. Nida, *Greek-English Lexicon of the New Testament: Based on Semantic Domains, Electronic Edition of the 2nd Edition, Volume 1* (New York: United Bible Societies, 1996), 466.

92   Ibid., 375.

93   P.L. Tan, *Encyclopedia of 7700 Illustrations: Signs of the Times* (Garland, TX: Bible Communications, Inc., 1996), 188.

94   J.P. Louw and E.A. Nida, *Greek-English Lexicon of the New Testament: Based on Semantic Domains, Electronic Edition of the 2nd Edition, Volume 1* (New York: United Bible Societies, 1996), 466.

95   C.R. Hebree in P.L. Tan, *Encyclopedia of 7700 Illustrations: Signs of the Times* (Garland, TX: Bible Communications, Inc., 1996), 908

96   Ibid., p. 1404.

CHAPTER 12

97   W.W. Wiersbe, *The Bible Exposition Commentary, Volume 2* (Wheaton, IL: Victor Books, 1996), 276.

98   M.G. Easton, *Easton's Bible Dictionary* (New York: Harper and Brothers, 1893).

99   W.W. Wiersbe, *The Bible Exposition Commentary, Volume 2* (Wheaton, IL: Victor Books, 1996), 281.

100   Ibid., 281.

[101] Ibid., 282.

[102] M. Henry, *Matthew Henry's Commentary on the Whole Bible: Complete and Unabridged in One Volume* (Peabody: Hendrickson, 1994), 2382.

CONCLUSION

[103] A.C. Myers, *The Eerdmans Bible Dictionary* (Grand Rapids, MI: Eerdmans, 1987), 1064.

About the Author

As a pastor, Rev. Lenn Zeller served four churches in three states (Ohio, Illinois and Pennsylvania) over a period of thirty-eight years. He also served the wider church on the denominational level in several capacities. Now retired, Rev. Zeller lives in the mountains of Pennsylvania, with his wife and partner of forty-five years, Janeen, and enjoys a more relaxed lifestyle. That added time has allowed him to write: first, *What God Has Said—About God,* and now *What God Has Said—About Jesus.* Both books in this series look to God's holy and eternal Bible for accurate and truthful answers about the person and character of God the Father and God the Son, Jesus. In an internet age when false perceptions and teachings thrive and multiply it seems all the more essential to focus on the clear teachings of the Word of God for clarity and genuine truth.

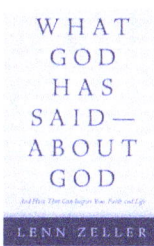

ALSO BY THIS AUTHOR:

What God Has Said—About God

Who is God? What is God really like? How are we to comprehend and understand an infinite, eternal, all-powerful Being who is the source and the purpose of all that exists? It's not enough to believe that God exists, we must have an accurate and realistic understanding of God if we are going to relate to Him in a meaningful and personal way. This book is written in an easy, readable style, and seeks to help people to have a correct understanding of the person and character of God, perhaps correcting some of the false views that are prevalent in today's post-Christian media culture. The book will be of interest to people of faith as they seek to grow in personal understanding and devotion, as well as to seekers who would like to know more about their Creator God. Questions for Consideration or Conversation at the end of each chapter allow for deeper individual reflection, or discussion in a small group setting. Available at: Amazon.com, BarnesandNoble.com, Christianbook.com and Westbowpress.com.

www.ingramcontent.com/pod-product-compliance
Lightning Source LLC
Chambersburg PA
CBHW070111080526
44586CB00013B/1260